Scrying

The Art of Seeing the Future
With Divination & Omens

by Dr. Shé D'Montford

ISBN: 978-0-994-35410-5
1st Edition
6th February 2011
© Shé D'Montford
Happy Medium Publishing
P.O. Box 3541
Helensvale Town Centre Qld.
Gold Coast
Australia
For World Wide Distribution

THE HAPPY MEDIUM PUBLISHING COMPANY
THE MESSAGE IS IN THE MEDIUM

Dr. Shé D'Montford's Little Book of :-
Scrying -
The Art of Seeing the Future
With Divination & Omens,
ISBN: 978-0-994-35410-5

Dr. Shé D'Montford's Little Book of Scrying - The Art of Seeing the Future With Divination & Omens, Graphic design & layout Shé D'Montford. Written By Rev. Dr. S. D'Montford © Copyright 6th February 2011 Gold Coast Australia. Published by Shambhallah Awareness Centre for educational purposes. **All Rights Reserved.** The information presented is protected under the Berne Convention for the Protection of Literature and Artistic works, under other international conventions and under national laws on copyright and neighbouring rights. Extracts of the information in this book may be reviewed, but not reproduced without express written permission from the publisher. Reproduction or translation of portions of this publication requires explicit, prior authorisation in writing. **Disclaimer:** The primary reason for this publication is entertainment and education about Pagan practices. While Shambhallah Awareness Centre has used all reasonable endeavours to ensure the information in this book is as accurate as possible, it gives no warranty or guarantee that the material, information, or publications made accessible by them are fit for any use whatsoever nor does that excuse you from using your common sense. Shambhallah Awareness Centre and Rev. Dr. S. D'Montford accepts no liability or responsibility for any loss or damage whatsoever suffered as a result of direct or indirect use or application of any material, publication or information obtained from them. **Quotes:** in tis book qualify as "fair use" under copyright law as use rationale, used for critical commentary and discussion by a non-profit organisation. Any other uses of these quotes may be copyright infringement.

Shambhallah Awareness Centre is a tax exempt Pagan Church and a not for profit organisation
 P.O. Box 3541, Helensvale Town Centre. Q. 4212
  http://www.shambhallah.org
  http://www.happymediumpublishing.org

Special Thanks to:-
Ken Wills, , Kushog, Kerry Kulkins,

THE HAPPY MEDIUM PUBLISHING COMPANY
THE MESSAGE IS IN THE MEDIUM

Contents: -

Scrying

1. Scrying
 on page 4
2. The Zi Gi Meditation
 on page 8
3. Crystal Ball Scrying
 on page 10
4. Tea & Coffee Cup Reading
 on page 12
5. Cloud Scrying
 on page 18
6. Fire Scrying
 on page 20
7. Water Scrying
 on page 22
8. Mirror Scrying
 on page 24
9. Chinese Ink Scrying
 on page 25
10. Other Forms of Divination
 on page 26

Omens

11. Animal Omens
 on page 38
12. Language of Bats
 on page 43
13. Augury
 on page 47
14. Language of Ravens & Crows
 on page 62
15. Owls Speak
 on page 70

Ancient Divination Systems

16. Ogham
 on page 78
17. Runes
 on page 83
18. Card Reading
 on page 95
19. Common Symbols & Meanings
 on page 100

Scrying

Scrying is the art of seeing and recognizing symbols and their meaning in the world around you.

Scrying is a group of *divination* forms, dating back thousands of years. Different modes of scrying have been used through out history in various civilizations across the world. Scrying is still actively used by many religious and spiritual beliefs systems. All indigenous cultures on every continent use some form of scrying in their spiritual rites and journeys, including the native Asians, Africans, Americans, Australians and Europeans.

It is also possible to see the future or prognosticate using scrying. It can show a querent their pastor present. Many great historical kings called upon "seers" to use different methods of scrying to aid them in battle or with love.

Some incorrectly think of scrying as being a skill that is exclusive to witchcraft; however, this is untrue. Several forms of divination are used in the Bible from Genesis to Revelations. Islamic cultures honour (scrying saved Mohammed's life as a child) it as does Judaism and Vedic culture.

Scrying can assist you in your daily life. It will help you understand you subconscious process and it will open up a dialog with the universe in which you can be an active participant.

You can use scrying to: -

* Gain Security

* Get answers

* Make difficult choices.

* Understand De Ja Vous

* See Future Events

* Know Outcomes

* Predict Rises & Falls

Anyone can perform scrying. Every one should. It is much better to open your eyes and try to see where you are going rather than stumble through life blindly and hope for the best. Using these techniques, you can begin to develop your own ability to directly see the future for yourself, so that you can be your own psychic.

We will discuss 20 simple scrying methods (and one that is a little more complex so that you can begin to stretch your skills) that you can begin to use today without any specialist training or the need for years of psychic development, such as: -

★Crystal Ball Gazing.
★Tea & coffee cup reading.
★Mirror Scrying.
★Cloud Scrying.
★Fire Scrying.
★Deep Water Scrying
★Oghams.

★Runes.
★Bird & Animal Omens.
★Card Reading
★Dream symbols
　　★and more

To perform these methods an understanding of basic symbology is required. At the end of this book is a list of symbols and their meanings. These symbols are commonly used by psychologists, Jungian analysts, dream interpreters, war propaganda agents, advertising agencies, academics and architects. These symbols transcend cultural boundaries and are a universal form of communication between humans. This is because symbols are the language used by our intelligent universe. We are hard wired to them. If we become aware of these symbols we can become aware of universal messages happening around us.

This book will give you a better understanding of those symbols, their uses, their meanings and how to relate them to your environment, Once you understand these symbols you can use the methods in this book to create a way to be clear and receptive to these messages, without the conscious mind doubting, fearing and sabotaging.

The techniques, methods and symbols that make up the scrying processes will become tools that you can access at any time and in any place, to help you get your needs met. Your world will become larger and more fulfilled. You will be more capable of avoiding the potholes in life's highway as you use scrying to open up a 2-way dialogue with the universe.

Escher - The Crystal Ball

The Zi Gi Meditation

To be able to see clearly and interpret clearly you must be able to push aside the chatter and clutter of daily life and find a clear calm poll of reflection inside of yourself. Once you are there you will be able to see the symbols signs and omens that are around you and inside your scrying tools. You will also be able to give an interpretation that is free from your own opinions. You can look up the interpretation of these symbols in the back of this book. The traditional method of the "Zi Gi" 10 X breath meditation is excellent for this.

This is the most basic and essential technique to employ when performing all scrying methods. Called "Zi Gi" it means "the Glorious Power of One Breath" in Tibetan. With the added meaning of "riding the wind horse" or controlling your own energy. The name sounds complicated but it has 3 simple steps.

Method:
1) 10 X Deep Breaths:
- Empty out your lungs to the absolute bottom. Till you almost feel like coughing. Then without holding your breath at the bottom, turn it around and breath in to the absolute top. Fill your lungs till you feel they may pop.
- No holding at the top or bottom - A continuous cycle.

2) 10 X Mantra.
- Use your favorite mantra, spell or affirmation. Alternatively use the "Ah" & "Om" sounds alternately, as low, long and as loud as is comfortable.

3) Then close and cross your eyes and focus on the point above and in the centre of your eyes.
- You will feel your focus shift and become very single pointed. This is called opening the 3rd eye.
- Then do 10 X deep breaths imagining breathing in through the soles of your feet and out through the third eye.
- Whist breathing in, draw in all the joy and goodness the earth has to offer.
- Whilst breathing out, release negativity and relax more and more with each exhalation also focusing on what you wish to create in your life.

If you have followed these steps as instructed, you will now be in the Theta brain wave state. The walking dream state. This is the state where images will form easily and you are consciously in contact with the flow of the subconscious mind.

This process should take 10-15 min. With practice you will be able to identify and gain this state with less breaths. After much practice you will find that you can attain this state with one deep focused breath.

This is the basic technique used for all scrying and is particularly effective with visual scrying methods such as crystal ball scrying, mirror scrying, fire scrying, cloud scrying, pond/lake scrying, and different forms of stone scrying and earth scrying.

With a little experimentation you will find the one that bests suits your soul and third eye - the one which is your favorite and with which you feel most connected.

Crystal Ball Scrying

Perhaps the best known form of scrying is crystal-ball gazing. This type of scrying became popular in the fifteenth century through out Europe. It can be done with any reflective spherical object. The crystal does not have to be clear some times colour or inclusions aid the images to form.

Glass, that has been purified by running lead through it during its molten state, is called "Lead Crystal." Natural crystal, that has been carved and polished into a ball, can add to the messages received. If you are using a natural crystal think of it as a living beings that will assist you to get results. Some people find this distracting and prefer to just use a pure clear glass sphere. Which you choose is a matter for your personal preferences. I suggest that at some time you try both so that you can feel the difference and see the different results that you will get.

By relaxing and peering into the crystal ball it is possible to see images take form within the crystal's many layers. These images are then interpreted by the scryer for themselves or for the querent/seeker who is asking the scryer questions.

Method:
- Clean the crystal ball and remove any smudges, marks or finger prints.
- Light a votive candle of any colour or of a colour aspected to the question asked.
    - **Red** - luck, home life, family matters, settling down, children.

- **Orange / Pink** - Sexual issues, crushes obsessions.
- **Yellow** - Fame recognition reward personal conflicts marriage engagements (Default colour for all future scrying)
- **Green / Gold** - Health, prosperity, love
- **Blue** - Communications, intellect, study, writing, technology.
- **Indigo** - Intuition, psychic development, seeing through deception.
- **Violet** - Connections and work with the divine.
- **Black and White** are neutral, and are often used for spirit communications.

- Do the Zi Gi.
- Relax and let the images form
- Do not judge or question the images - just observe.
- Check the meaning of any images or symbols against the list in the back of this book.

Tea & Coffee Cup Reading

Tasseomancy or tea-leaf divination, is a form of divination associated with the Gypsies and the English. Yet scrying from tea leaves has been around as long as there has been tea. The Eastern world has been using tea for more than 4500 years. Tea was only introduced into the West a relatively recent 400 years ago. The Chinese, who are well known for seeking omens, paid attention to the dregs of their cups for symbols or unusual patterns.

According to legend tea leaf reading began with the very discovery of the beverage. Chinese Emperor, Shan Nong, in 2737 B.C. had a habit of boiling his drinking water. One day while he was enjoying the country side, he left his cup stand. When he returned to it, a few leaves from a near by camellia bush had fallen into his boiling water by chance. He was about to throw it out when he was fascinated to notice the image of a strong healthy man drinking from a cup was formed by the leaves in the bottom of his cup. He sniffed at the brew which gave off a rich, alluring aroma, so he drank it and found it to be refreshing and energizing. He immediately gave the command that the bushes be cultivated in the gardens of his palace for the duel purpose of brewing and divination.

Success in this divinatory art is often attributed to the seer's ability to see the symbols and work with their intuition and clairvoyance.

You will need:
- A teapot with freshly brewed loose leaf tea in it
  or

- 1/2 a teaspoon of loose leaf tea & Boiling water

- A cup and saucer.

- A quiet and peaceful atmosphere is highly conducive to a good tea reading and it is comforting to the client.

Method:
- The pot should be brewed upon the arrival of the seeker.
or
- They place the spoon of tea into the cup.

- If the leaves spill for the cup or the pot it is considered very fortunate.

- The seeker should be seated as near to the reader as possible

- The brew is pored or boiling water is now added and the seeker stirs the cup and focuses on the future or their question while stirring it. (Do not stir another person's tea as it can bring on an argument.)

- Bubbles floating to the top means a kiss or money coming to the seeker.

- A stalk or full leaf floating to the surface indicates a visitor:- A hard stem is a man and a soft one a woman.

- To find out how many days until the visitor arrives, place the wet leaf or stalk on the back of your hand, turn you hand sideways and tap it with the other hand until it falls off. 1 tap = 1 day

- The seeker then drinks the tea but leaves a small amount in the bottom of the cup.

- The longer the seeker holds the cup and concentrates, the better the reading will be.

- If the tea is too strong it shows a new friendship in the future but if it is too weak it indicates the end of one.

- The residue in the cup should be swirled three times clockwise by the seeker.

- Holding both cup and saucer in each hand, the seeker must then touch the edge of the saucer with the cup, wish a wish of the heart, and turn the cup over immediately onto the saucer.

- This allows the liquid to drain away and the leaves stick to the cup.

- It is then passed to the reader. The reader takes the cup with her right hand.

- The area near the handle inside the teacup, represents the seeker or their work or business.

- The near, inner side of the cup indicates their fortune.

- The far side of the cup indicate thoughts and issues that remain unsorted.

- If there is sadness in the seekers future, the tears or drops of tea, will not drain away.

- If a star appears at the top of the cup then wishes will be fulfilled. If not they wont.

- It is standard practice to view the cup as a time period of one month.

- Things that are half way up will occur in two weeks, further down in three to four weeks.

- The top represents today and the rim is now.

- Symbols right at the rim represent "first thing in the morning."

- If it is a whole leaf or stalk at the rim it will be shocking news.

- Anything pooling at the bottom of the cup represents problems and is also timed as now.

- The size and clearness of the image or symbol is very important. The larger and clear the greater the magnitude of what the symbol indicates will occur.

- If the symbol disappears immediately after being read, it is indicative of things that are starting to no longer matter or be of significance.

- Inside the cup, stalks and sprigs represent people - tightly curled ones are male and loosely curled ones are female.

- Stalks that are standing upright, represent straightforward people. Unless there is some type of a weapon around them, then it is a warning to be careful of them.

- Crossed stalks indicate people who are annoyed and frustrated. Symbols nearby will indicate why.

- Sideways stalks represent untrustworthy people.

- Once the reading is done throw the tea leaves onto the ground near the front door to ward off evil spirits or place them at the back of the fireplace wood stove or BBQ (hearth) to ward off poverty.

Coffee Grounds
Coffee divination is thought to have come from Turkey.

General coffee cup scrying is very similar to scrying tea leaves. It is done with freshly brewed ground coffee. It can be performed in any café for your friends and clients. The fine powdered dregs can produce clear images and symbols. The methods used for the reading and the meaning of the symbols are very similar to those used for tea (however there are no floating objects or stalks.) As with tea, you can look up the interpretation of coffee symbols in the back of this book.

Here is an Italian version of how to do a coffee cup reading that is a little different.
Method:
- Put 2 teaspoonfuls of coffee into a filter, pour on boiling water, and place the filter in a safe place.

- Leave it there for 2-3 days, until the dregs dry completely. Then move the dregs to a shallow saucepan

- Pour on a small glass of cold water

- Place the vessel on the stove and let the water heat slowly. Allow to reduce.

- Remove the saucepan right before boiling point.

- Turn the contents out onto a flat white plate.

- Gently shake the plate and blow upon it, until the grounds separate themselves from the water and coagulate.

- Then leave the plate to dry for half an hour.

- The coffee grounds will have formed symbols whilst drying. Get a magnifying glass and look closely at the symbols.

- You can look up the interpretation of these symbols in the back of this book.

Cloud Scrying

Laying on the beach and enjoying the morphing pictures formed by the clouds is a very ancient form of scrying. The Celtic Druids would look to the clouds for spiritual insight in battles, for spiritual rites, and for the harvest. This was called "Air Scrying."

Children love doing this and it can be a way to make them aware of their spiritual power very early in life.

Method:
- The secret to successful cloud scrying is to be totally relaxed.
- Let the interpretations of the symbols flow and float as easily through your mind as the clouds through the sky.
- Allow your intuition to have full say when interpreting the symbols that you see.

For instance, if I am thinking about my business and I notice a cloud that looks like an eagle's head, it could indicate for me to increase my market to the US. Eagles are blessings from the gods and good things on the way.

Cloud Vaporizing - Creating Your future

Always remember this:

> *A person controls their fate*
> *Their fate does not control the person*

If you have seen something in the clouds that may indicate a bad situation ahead this is one of many techniques you can use to make bad luck vaporize (along with the cloud image that is indicating it.) If you can make that cloud disappear then you will be able to turn away from the path that is not good for you. If the cloud persists and wont dissolve then you may not be able to avoid this situation. In that case use the information shown to you to prepare. If you are ready for it you can make the most of of a bad situation.

For instance there were many signs to indicate the economic downturn in 2009-2013. Lack of clouds and long term drought were good indicators that his was on its way. My clients who listened to my warnings were able to clear their debit and cash up, ready to increase their assets as others who did not listen were forced to sell theirs.

Method:
- Locate a small cloud

- Do the Zi Gi Meditation

- Focus all your intent with your out breath through the third eye on vaporizing that cloud.

- Di this Zi Gi with you eyes open watching the cloud. Concentrate with your eyes

- Continue to visualize breathing out of your third eye and blowing the cloud away like blowing a candle flame out.

- Say to your self:
	"Make it evaporate, make it disappear."

- Don't let that dark cloud out of your sight until it is gone.

Fire Scrying

Watching a fire in a fireplace on a cold winter's evening is relaxing and hypnotic. It warms the body and lulls the conscious mind thus freeing the subconscious to perceive messages that the busy work-a-day mind ignores. Many have experienced spontaneous revelations whilst staring into an open fire or candle flame.

Fire is about passion and things that consume you. It is a good scrying method for finding out about love and personal interests that you are passionate about.

Method:
Sit in front of a fire or votive candle, (See the section on colours of votive candles in the crystal ball scrying section.) at a safe distance from sparks and radiance burns until you are warm, relaxed and your mind has stilled to the clear calm pool of reflection.
- Close your eyes
- Do the Zigi
- Open your eyes.
- Look directly into the flames and burning embers.
- Don't strain your eyes; blink normally.
- Breathe deeply.
- What images, shapes and symbols do you perceive in the fire, flame and embers.
- When you get up to mover, write down whatever images form in the flames and have stuck in your mind.
- Check the symbols for their meanings with our list in the back of this book.

Fire Oracle

Fire is not just destructive it can be used to create and release the energy of your wishes into the universe as heat and smoke.

You will need:
- Flame
- A piece of paper to write on. (Chinese joss paper from you local Chinese grocer is very good.)
- A Saucer.

Method:
- Write your wish on a piece of paper.
- Place it into a fire or flame with the writing face downwards. When it burns too much to hold it drop the paper into the fire or onto a readied saucer.
- If the paper is entirely consumed, your wish will come true.
- If only the part written on is consumed, your wish will be delayed.
- However, if the writing remains, you will not get what you want.

For better results:
Try creating a sacred starter flame for your candle or fire. Use the concentrated heat of the sun through a magnifying glass or a crystal ball to light some kindling to start your fire. The energy of a fire started from the sun will be much better than one started with a disposable cigarette lighter.

Water Scrying

Sitting by a clear pool of water, a pond, a lake or a dock over looking some still deep seawater is a favorite way for many people to meditate. It can help you to become calm and still. It is a way of connecting with the deep subconscious and can therefore be used as a tool for scrying. Gaelic cultures consider creatures in close connection with water to be dwellers of the psychic realm Their words for "The Second Sight," the scryers gift, and "Deep Water" are interchangeable. *An Da Shealladh* is believed to have originally been the name of a Celtic goddess of second sight, *deep* darkness or *deep* water.

(Yes -the Gaelic word "An Da Shealladh" pronounced - an-da-shé-alla is a contributing factor to the naming of Shambhallah Awareness Centre - it means "those with the second sight.")

A word of caution when doing deep water scrying. It will bring up answers to questions from deep within you, possibly from places that you may have hidden long ago and may not want to look. However it is beneficial to use water scrying if you want to see other peoples true motivations as it reveals things deeply hidden. It can help you catch out liars, cheats and thieves.

The Water Oracle

Water can be used for more than just a scrying method. It can also be an accurate oracle, answering questions with a clear yes or no.

Method:
Concentrate on your question. Repeat it in your mind several times, then drop a small stone or pebble into still

water. If the number of the ripples is odd, the answer is "yes," if it's even, the answer is "no."

Full Moon Water / Mirror Divination

You will need:
- A bright, shiny silver coin.
- A natural body of water or your scrying mirror or a small, black bowl filled with water.

Method:
- Perform this ceremony outside at night where the rays of the Moon can reflect directly into the water or mirror.
- If you cannot go outside a darkened room, position yourself near a window that the Moon shines through will do
- Place the coin in the water or take the mirror or water
- Perform the Zigi
- Repeat the ancient spell below from *"The "Aradia"* as your mantra:-

> *"'Moon, Moon, beautiful Moon!*
> *Fairer far than any star;*
> *Moon, O Moon, if it may be,*
> *Bring good fortune unto me!'*
> (If you can, try the original Italian version below it is very powerful. If not the English version will suffice)
> > *'Luna mia, bella Luna!*
> > *Più di una altra stella;*
> > *Tu sei sempre bella!*
> > *Portatemi la buona fortuna!'*

- Gaze deeply into the water or the mirror.
- Allow any images to flow through your vision.
- Look up the meaning of the symbols in the back of this book.

Mirror Scrying

Magical people have used mirrors for visions and insight into the future, since their invention. Black mirrors are especially favored for scrying. Legend says that the Goddess Hecaté created the first black mirror. Breaking a silver backed scrying mirror is where the superstition about 7 years of back luck from breaking a mirror originated. It is indeed very bad luck to break a magickal mirror. It is an invaluable tool. The Disney movie "Snow White and the Seven Dwarfs" crudely misrepresented the scrying mirror's powers and have made people afraid of it - Yet it is a very useful tool and should not be avoided because of childhood fears from cartoon characters.

Method:
- Darken the room and try to make it silent.
- Light one votive candle. (See the section on colour of votive candles in the Crystal Ball Scrying section.)
- Perform the Zi Gi meditation.
- Think of the mirror as a living being that will be giving you the visions.
- Look up any images or symbols that you see in the back of this book.

Mirror scrying is a form of water scrying. The ancients equated mirrors with captured water. Performing a mirror scrying or water divination ritual by light of the full moon can be very powerful. It can be a deeply mystical experience, as using the moon's light to reveal the images in your magick mirror can produce startling results. (See the "Full Moon Divination" in the previous section.)

Chinese Ink Scrying

Gazing into a saucer of inky water is a favorite form of scrying in Asia. The methods is very similar to mirror scrying except that you make your own ink.

To make your ink:
- Chinese ink is a mixture of soot and water.
- To gather usable soot, take a metal or white porcelain saucer and hold it inverted over a burning candle flame. Black soot will form on it in swirls.

- Turn over the saucer and pour in a small amount of water.
- Swirl the water 3 times clockwise. Not enough to completely mix the soot and water into ink, just enough to allow ink to swirl and form symbols

- Follow the steps for the mirror scrying method.

Other Forms of Divination

The Paper Oracle

Even paper can be used as an oracle!
This is a method for getting quick answers

You will need:
- A large empty bucket,
- A bucket full of water
- 13 pieces of paper exactly the same size and colour. I use rice joss paper from my local Chinese grocery store. These papers are natural, traditional and usually small enough so that you don't have to cut them. They can be left to dissolve in the water or poured out on the garden where they make great compost.

Method:
- Write simple outcomes for your troubling question on each piece of paper.

- An uncomplicated yes/no style answer is the best.

- Place the pieces of paper at the bottom of the empty bucket. Do not fold them. It makes them too hard to read when they are wet.

- Rapidly pour the water from the full bucket into the empty bucket.

- The first paper that rises to the surface has the answer you need.

Black and White Squares

Method:
- Get two large squares of paper the same size.
- One should be coloured black and one white.
- Go to a high place.
- Concentrate on your question.
- Throw the squares out at the same time.
- If the black square reaches the ground first, the answer to your question is "no," if the white, "yes."

Dandelion Divination

Dandelions are very popular as oracles. As children we are told to make wishes by blowing on a dandelion.

- If all the seeds fly off in one breath, your wish will almost immediately come true.
- If some seeds remain, it will be delayed.
- If many seeds are left, you will probably not obtain your wish.

Wedding Ring Oracles

- Take any gold wedding ring and attach it to a black cotton thread.

- Grasp the thread between the thumb and first finger of the left hand and hold the ring over a glass of water.

- Concentrate on your question.

- Then release the thread.

- The ring will fall to the bottom of the glass.

- If it falls to the left side of the glass, the answer to your question is "no"

- If it falls to the right side, "yes".

- However, if the ring touches either the front or back of the glass then it is not a proper time to ask your question.

- Try again after at least a day or two.

Human Body Scrying

Being aware of what your body is telling you can be an accurate oracle. For instance: - Feeling depressed for no apparent reason means unexpected good news!

Ears
- **Small** A generous person
- **Curled**: Long life

- **Big lobes:** A lucky person
- **Ringing in the right ear** foresees pleasant news,
- **Ringing in the left ear** means bad news.

Itching
- **Head:** Receiving money. Getting riches.
- **Left side of Head**: Meeting a strange man
- **Right side of Head**: Meeting a strange Woman
- **Crown of head**: Advance in position.

Cheek
- **Right cheek**: Someone is speaking well of you. Praise
- **Left cheek**: Someone is gossiping about you. Blame

Eye
- **Right Eye**: You will laugh
- **Left Eye**: You will cry
- **Right eye**/eyebrow: You will meet an old friend.
- **Left eye**/eyebrow: Great disappointment.

Nose
- **Nose** (inside): Sorrow.
- **Nose** (outside): You will be kissed, annoyed or shake hands with a fool

Lips
- **Top Lip**: Someone is talking about you with disrespect.
- **Bottom Lip**: You will be kissed.

Hands
- **Right palm**: Receiving money.
- **Left Palm**: Giving money

Sole of foot: You will walk over strange ground

Birthmarks and Moles
- The greater the size of the mole or birthmark, the greater will be the force of the omen associated with it.
- A round mole is fortunate,
- Irregular moles are bad luck.
- An oval mark is moderately fortunate.
- Light-colored moles are good,
- Dark ones are unfortunate.
- The more hairs there are on a mole, the more unfortunate is its meaning.

Abdomen: Can indicate a greedy and selfish person.

Ankle: Man, refinement. Woman, great energy and independence.

Arm
- **Right**: Wisdom; Success
- **Left:** Argumentative; financial problems
- **Arm hole**: Riches and Honour

Back: An open and honest person with a bit of arrogance and sensuality.

Breast: On the left side means success in undertakings. In the center means the person will never enjoy opulence but will never want for the necessities of existence. On the right side shows that person will suffer extremes of fortune.

Cheek:
- **Right cheek** foretells a happy marriage; the nearer it is to the mouth, the greater will be the wealth and happiness of the person.

- **Left cheek** however denotes financial difficulties.

- **Chin**: Your undertakings will be successful always'

Ear
- **Right side**: Wealth & Honour
- **Left Side**. Poverty & Dishonor

- **Foot**:
- **Right foot:** A great love for traveling and change.
- **Left foot:** An intellectual and intelligent person

Forehead:
- **Right side:** the mole means you have great mental power.
- **Left side:** it means you're extravagant and spend more money than you actually have!

Hands - Will have lots of children

Lip: Great Talker

Middle section of the face: A mole anywhere in the middle section of the face - between the outer edge of the eyebrows from the forehead to the chin, denotes a person who is extremely attractive to others and may have many love affairs.

Neck & Stomach: Strength

Throat: Riches and Health

Sneezing

A series of sudden unexpected natural sneezes, (not induced by chemicals in the air, illness or drugs), from a healthy person, is a barometer of immanent weather change. The more sneezes the bigger the change.

Ancient Germanic cultures believed that sneezing expelled evil spirits from the body. Saying: "Gesundheit " to the sneezer which literally means *"Gods health you,"* is a way to bless the person and ward off the return of any evil whilst the sneezer's body is defenseless during and just after sneezing. Also, the sneezing sound, "kash shoo," sounds very like the English words "curse you." Saying : "Bless you," counteracts this.

- If you sneeze on Monday, you sneeze for danger;
- Sneeze on a Tuesday, kiss a stranger;
- Sneeze on a Wednesday, sneeze for a letter;
- Sneeze on a Thursday, something better;
- Sneeze on a Friday, sneeze for sorrow;
- Sneeze on a Saturday, joy to-morrow.
- Sneeze on a Sunday, your safety seek-

The devil will have you the whole of the week.
- Unless you sneeze during Sunday morning's fasting.

Then you will enjoy true love everlasting.

Counting Sneezes
One for sorrow, two for joy,
Three for a girl, for a boy,
Five for silver, six for gold,
Seven for a secret, never to be told,
Eight for a wish, nine for a kiss,
Ten for a time of joyous bliss.

Weather Omens

The traditional weather omens and proverbs given below have been collected from different parts of Europe. These are perhaps the most accurate of omens.

Sun: When the sun is covered with a haze, expect bad weather. When it goes down in dark and heavy clouds, the morrow will be wet. If the sun comes out while it is still raining rain will continue for a few more days.
*"If red the sun begins his race be sure the rain will fall space;
If the sun goes pale to bed 't`will rain tomorrow, it is said."*

Moon:
- If the moon is encircled by a single ring, it is an indication of rain, even in fine weather.
- When the yellow full moon rises into a clear sky on the horizon, a short time of fine weather is announced.
- If the full moon rises red, it is a sign of the wind.

Stars: When they flicker and appear larger than usual, wet weather is in store.

Clouds:
*"A mackerel sky
   Twelve hours dry."
"Clouds floating high
   Will soon run dry."*

Sky:
*"Red sky at night
Sailors delight
Red sky at morning
Sailors warning*

Wind:
*"Wind is in the north,
Hail comes forth,
Wind is in the west,
Blows strong & wet
Wind is in the east,
Not good for man nor beast,*

> *Wind east of west,
> Is a sign of a blast,
> Wind north or south,
> Is a sign of a drought,*

*When the wind is in the north,
   The skillful fisher goes not forth."*

Myomancy

Have you ever had a mouse or a rat go out of its way to chew something unusual of yours?

Why is this so?

Maybe that little mouse has a message for you and is trying to get your attention. According to Herodotus, Sennacherib's attempt to invade Egypt was thwarted due to his army's weapons being systematically destroyed by rats the night before they were due to attack.

Myomancy is the practice of reading omens from the behavior of rats or mice. From myo for "mouse" + mancy for "divination."

Mouse or rat cries and their unusually selective destructive habits have historically been seen as a warning to not proceed with a certain course of action.

Ælain relates that Fabius Maximus resigned his dictatorship as a consequence of a "warning" from these creatures; Varro reports that Cassius Flaminius retired from the command of the cavalry for the same reason.

Early mariners observed that rats would sense the sinking of a ship before anyone else could realize it and make for safety and land. They would appear out of the bilges and run across the decks in a thundering herd before the ship had begun to founder.

In modern times rat and mice have been observed leaving natural disaster sites such as earthquake, tsunami, flood and fire areas in droves, hours or even days before the disaster.

Myomancy was referred to in the bible at Isaiah 66:17. The Hebrew word for "mouse" is derived from a root meaning "to separate, divide, or judge."

An Egyptian manuscript in the Bibliothèque Nationale de France in Paris contains the representation of a soul going to judgement in which one of the figures is depicted with the head of a rat wearing a traditional judges' wig.

Mouse Scrying

Do you have a mouse in your house?
If so you can use it for this divination method.

You will need:
- 2 small bowls

- 2 plates of fine sand

- 1 small piece of fresh bread

- 1 small piece of stale bread

Method:
- Place the 2 plates of fine sand near where you feel your mouse is hiding.

- Place 1 small bowl on to the centre of each plate

- Place the fresh bread into one and the stale bread in the other.

- Leave undisturbed for several hours to 1 day.

- If the Mouse has taken the fresh bread your answer is yes!

- If the mouse has taken the stale bread then your answer is no!

- If The mouse has taken both, there will be good success but not with out a few hassles.

- Observe the mouse tracks in the plates of fine sand.

- Can you perceive and symbols or even letters spelt out in the sand by the mouse tracks?

- These can give you details about the eventuality of the question you asked.

- Look up the meaning of any symbols in the back of this book

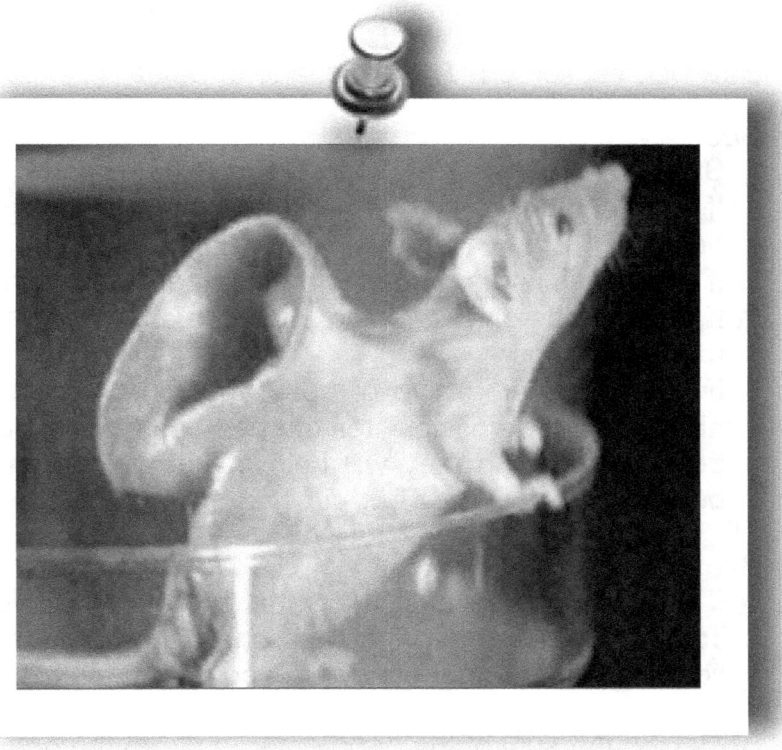

Are you listening for messages from the mice?

Other Animal Omens

Is there a deeper meaning to encounters with certain animals that you do not usually see in your daily life?

Ants - busy climbing up high - bad weather or floods.

Ass or donkey: If it is coming from the opposite direction, it is a bad omen.
> Hark! I hear the asses bray.
> We shall have some rain today.

Bat: See section on "The Language of Bats>"

Bee:
- Staying in the hive - a period of rain is coming
- If a bee lands on your head you will rise to great heights
- If a bee flies into a room it is an omen of good news
- If a bee lands on a sleeping baby, the child is destined for great things.
- If you live near a hive of bees you must keep them abuzz with the gossip. - tell the bees any family news, good or bad and they will help make it work out the best way for you and your family.

Beetle
- If you see a beetle on its back it is lucky to flip it over
- To kill a beetle is bad luck and can bring thunder and lightning. Remember they were sacred in Egypt.

Butterfly: the soul of the dead emerges from the body as a butterfly -
- Therefore it is lucky to see a butterfly particularly a white one.

- Killing a butterfly brings bad luck

Carp - Good luck. Keep a scale from a carp that you eat at New Years in your purse and it won't be empty all year.

Cat:
- To kill a cat brings complete misfortune. The ancient Egyptians punished that crime by death!
- To tread on a cat's tail is a little unfortunate.
- If a cat suddenly abandons the house of its masters, there will be a great disaster in that house soon.
- A black cat is good luck, unless it crosses your path or stares at you for a long period of time. If you see a black cat on the road stop and wait for another car to pass you.
- If a tortoiseshell cat wonders into your home it is good luck
- If a cat sneezes bad weather is on the way.
- If it sits with its back to the fire - storm warning.
- If a cat washes its face by rubbing its paw over its ear and down onto its face - fine weather on the way
- Tabby cat with an "M" on their forehead are luck because they were blessed by Mohammad as his favorite animal.

Cow:
- Cows laying down in a field - wet weather on the way.
- Cows under a tree - it will be a hot day
- A cow breaking into an enclosed garden is bad luck
- Where a cow leave a cow pat it blesses that earth.

Dog:
- If a dog howls outside your house for no apparent reason, there will be death in the neighborhood.
- If it digs a hole in your garden it is bad luck

- If a strange dog follows and is friendly towards you, this is very good luck.

Ferret: Your enterprise will be successful!

Fox - to see one is lucky to see many is unlucky.

Goat: An omen of prosperity.

Hare:
- Unlucky for pregnant women to sight one.
- Omen that you predictions for the future will come true.
- To carry a hare's foot brings good luck.
- If a hare runs across your path retrace your steps.

Horse:
- To meet a piebald horse brings good fortune, spit on the ground and wish.
- If lovers meet a white horse, they will be happy together.
- Yet, a bride and groom should not have a marriage coach drawn by 2 white horses
- Gamblers like racehorses with white stockings on their for leg but it is unlucky if it has one white stocking on it back leg and one on one of its fore legs.
- stormy weather is on it s way if horses stand with their backs to a wall or hedge.

Ladybird :
An oracle insect. If you find one place it on the back of your hand and say one of these verses:
>*Fly ladybird North, South, East or West*
>*Fly to the one that I love the best.*

Then throw it into the air and watch which way it goes.

Ladybird, ladybird, fly away home
Your house is on fire and your children all gone

Watch which direction it flies and this is the direction the rain will come from.

Lamb:
- If the first lamb of the season that you see is facing you it is luck if you have some money in your pockets.
- If the Lambing season begins with twins it is a very good omen for the whole country side.

Lizard: If you see a lizard in an unusual place, then disappointment is on its way!

Mouse: See the section on "Myomancy"
- If the mouse is white, you will be happy in love, especially if received as a gift.
- A brown mouse is propitious but in a less degree.
- A gray mouse indicates danger.

Pig: A pig is very unlucky.
- If a wedding party returning from church meets a wandering pig, the couple will have an unhappy marriage.
- Fisherman think that if anybody says the word pig on the boat the catch will be poor.
- If fisherman see a pig cross their path on their way to their boat it is a bad omen.
- To avert illness walk three times around a pigsty and spit each time

Rabbit: Miners dislike seeing a rabbit on their way to work as they feel it could indicate bad luck for the day.

Sheep: If you meet a flock of sheep on the road it is lucky to move through the middle to part them.

Snake:
- To dream of snakes is about acquiring wisdom. It is lucky.
- A passive non-moving, non-aggressive, non-afraid snake around you is very lucky.
- If the snake is coming towards you, treachery will be directed towards you.
- If the snake is going away from you, you will harm your enemies soon.

Spider
If a ver small spider fall on you especially on your hands, money is coming to you - hence "money spider."
If you want to live and thrive
Let a spider run alive

Toad: Lucky for a bride if she meets on on the way to church

Tortoise: An omen of tranquility and support. A creature long associated with divination and good omens. If you get a chance to stare at the tortoise or turtle shell long enough, You can use it for divination. Look up any symbols or image you see formed within the striations of its shell in the back of this book

The Lo Shu oracle tortoise gave us the symbols of the I-Ching, "The Book of Changes" a complex Chinese oracle system and a system of magic square mandalas. - Image Credit: Jain

The Language of Bats

Bats, like crows, are otherworldly creatures that dwell in our physical plane. As such they are maligned and misunderstood.

Because a flight of bats works so perfectly in unison they have been associated with shape shifters that can change their shape into a group of bats or a fog or a wolf. Several smaller varieties of bats are parasitical; as such, they have long been associated with the legends of vampires, rabies, disease, death and ghosts. In Western Culture, the bat is symbolic of the night and its foreboding nature. Yet in Chinese lore the bat symbolises longevity and happiness and to the Polish, Macedonians and Gypsies, the bat is considered lucky. To the North American Apache, Cherokee and Creek, the bat is the trickster spirit, like the coyote. Bosnians, Tongans and West Africans considered bat to be the physical manifestation of a separable soul, similar to the way the ancients Greeks viewed the butterfly.

Ozzy Osborne was not the first to bite the heads off live bats. 20,000 years ago, according to the Binbinga of northern Australia, Ulanji, a snake ancestor was said to have climbed rocks in order to bite the heads off flying foxes. They were a major food source for traditional Australian Aborigines who hunted them with boomerangs. In their legend, they are the only creatures to travel to the land of the Setting Sun and meet their dead ancestors, in which they use their leather and bark like wings as protection against enemies and blood sucking parasites.

However, eating bats is now prohibited in Australia, as they are a protected species. In the United Kingdom all bats are protected under the Wildlife and Countryside Acts; therefore disturbing a bat or its roost can result in a heavy fine.

Bats can tell people about learning to sense their way through the darkness, to come out reborn leaving behind the old self, old habits, and old behaviours. Tarot card 12, the hanged man symbolises this, just as before a human baby is born, the baby hangs upside down in the mother's womb, waiting for the birthing process to take place. You may have found that if a bat has come before you that you have been going through a dark time in your life when you must let go of who you used to be in order to become who you desire to be. Where the butterfly is a manifestation of your psyche, the bat is a manifestation of the psychopomps, the one who takes you on an initiatory journey of transformation. The bat is asking you to go beyond sight when you are blindfolded by the darkness, a blinded child of humanity in the initiation process. With her big sonic echo-locating ears she is asking us to listen. Get quiet, listen to your soul calling to you from the darkness and listen to the message that she has for you.

Bats have a clear and precise language as they live in large communities as we humans do. Though not often seen, when they present themselves to our attention they are often trying to communicate important messages to poor ignorant self-isolating humans. If you take the time to begin to understand their language they can reveal the hidden mysteries.

Bat Omens
- Suddenly finding a colony of bats under a house or in a cave or on a bush-walk- Carefully hidden secrets will be revealed – increase in intuition.

- Bat flies across water – Ease, abundance, better times

- Bat flies into you home – Hidden fears – bad choices – choosing the wrong path

- Bat eating in your yard - Trust – you are being given the ability to change into something new.

- Travelling and suddenly coming across the pungent smell of Flying Foxes – Something will change on this journey

- Bat gets tangled in you hair – If easily untangled a tricky problem will be sorted out quickly - If it has to be cut out – bad Omen – Loss of power

- Bat flies around you at night - Your intuition and senses will increase

- Dead bat found - Rare and lucky - Remove that heart if possible put it in salt dry it out and keep it in a small salt bag. This will bring you luck in card games and other games of chance. See "Bat Luck Spell."

- A colony of bats crosses your path - During the day - Working as a team will over come you problems – During the night - Be cautious if you are alone

- Seeing a flight of bats crossing the sky at sunset - Abundance and plenty

- Seeing a flight of bats cross the sky at sunrise – A lost opportunity

© Copyright Rev. Dr. S. D'Montford Wednesday, February 21, 2007 Gold Coast Australia

Bat's Heart Luck Spell

As Batman says: "Bats are great little survivors." It is most unusual to find one of these little guys' dead as their sonar combined with their quick reflexes usually allows them to react quickly enough to avoid any potentially harmful situation. Their response time is prompted by their ability to rapidly raise their heart rate almost instantly to 1400 beats per minute Yet it may slow to 20 beats per minute when resting.

To find a dead bat is a rare and lucky thing. Remove that heart if possible cover it in salt for a few weeks to dry it out. This charm is said to attract good luck when playing games of chance, such as cards or lotteries. When the heart is dry wrap a red silk ribbon around it and carry the bat's heart folded into a silk handkerchief. Some people believe that just tying the silk string around a bat's heart will bring money. Keep your little luck bundle in a wallet or pocket when you are having a flutter. You can also use a red silk ribbon to tie it to the hand used for dealing cards.

Carry the heart in a green cloth bag and anoint it with protection oil for optimum financial results.

Augury
The Secret Language of Birds

For thousands of years, cultures have used birds as omens. Bird images permeate the human psyche and speak directly to our subconscious. The Greeks and Romans believed that the Gods took on the guise of winged creatures. Thus the study of the chattering, singing, feeding and flight of birds, Augury, became an art form and was used to foretell future events and receive guidance. Nothing official was undertaken in the classical period unless the birds sanctioned it. Augury was held to ensure the best timing for the installment of new government leaders This is the meaning of the word in'augur'ation.

Socrates was also a big believer in augury. "...Socrates said what he meant: for he said that the deity gave him a sign. Many of his companions were counseled by him to do this or not to do that in accordance with the warnings of the deity: and those who followed his advice prospered, and those who rejected it had cause for regret." (Xenophon)

Augury: The art of foretelling the future with bird signs and omens is credited to Tiresias, blind prophet of Thebes, who was taught the language of the birds by Athena, the goddess of wisdom through her pet Owl.

An ancient augury session may take hours or days of observation, before delivering a verdict. The augur would ask yes or no questions after which everything in that area was noted. The kind of birds, the birds sounds, the direction they were flying, if they made any changes of direction as well as the weather and cloud formations and all the natural phenomenon.

Yet today we can receive quick responses by just noticing the behavior of the birds around us. It can be natures way of delivering a little winged message. Crows are well known for their ability to be divine messages to humans. Crows enjoy communication with humans. The more attention you give to them they more messages they will try to deliver to you but more on crows later. However, all birds can bring you a message. Noting the type or number of birds can communicate the significance of the message. Keeping a journal of which birds you notice and their meanings, can be a good way of seeing the accuracy of your interpretation of the messages that the universe is trying to deliver to you. Maybe the Greeks were onto something, and the gods do try to speak to us through birds!

Bird Omens

Birds omens are broadly divided into two classes:

- **Oscines**, those giving auguries by their calls

- **Alites**, those giving auguries just by sighting them or by their flight path."

　　　　　　　Here are some examples:-

Alites

- **Birds flying into houses** were such bad omens in ancient Greece that they would capture these birds and hang them outside their doors to atone for "those evils which they threatened the family"
- **Birds seen on your left**, especially dark birds, indicate bad luck.
- **Crow**: unfavorable when it was seen on the left.
- **Birds on the right** are, however, a fortunate sign.
- **Raven**: a favorable omen when it appeared on the right.
- Birds flying **from the left-hand side to the right** are fortunate, Birds flying **from right to left** across the observer's path are an omen of ill luck.
- If the birds fly **straight towards you**, they will bring good luck to you,
- If a **flock of birds** flies about a person, it is an excellent omen for them.
- If they're **flying away from you**, they can take happiness with them!

"Plainly, however, it is based on the Pythagorean doctrine of "Opposites," in which the Odd (number) *is "superior" to the Even, and the "Right"* (side) *to the Left. In Greek augury, also, the left was the side of ill omen."* (Plato in Twelve Volumes)

Oscines

If the bird sings or utters as it flies, it means there is still hope.
However if the bird heard was a raven, a rook, a crow or any bird of prey, then this is a bad omen.
Raven: Pliny says that the worst message is when

ravens "make a plaintive whine, as though they were being strangled." (*Natural History X.33*)

Any bird **tearing themselves** is not favorable for the person who sites it.

Military Men and Naval Officers still watch for bird sign during conflict. Here are some of the things they watch for:-

- **Dove or Crane** brings a period of peace for Kings or generals

- **Swallows** were unlucky

- **Vultures** meant slaughter if following an army.

- **Ravens** and **crows** were also dangerous for armies; Alexander the Great's death was preceded by ravens.

- **Owls** portended victory.

- **Cocks crowing** were auspicious.

- **Hen** crowing is very rare and is considered a very bad judgment.

- **Swan** at sea is an unfavorable sighting for mariners.

- **Albatross** is good luck if it lands on your ship at sea, though this can indicate a storm. Sailors will often touch their little gold cross that they keep on their person when they sight one and wish it no ill. It is a symbol of survival at sea as an albatross can live for years on the sea without setting foot on land if it sets foot on a ship this is a rare thing indeed. Thus it is very bad luck to kill an albatross as this is believed it will curse the ship and all who sail upon it. The word 'albatross' is sometimes used metaphorically to mean a psychological burden that feels like a curse.

- If a bird or flock of **birds suddenly change direction** in mid flight, and you see this, you must be on your guard against danger or surprise attack by your adversary.

- If the bird you are observing **hovers** while on wing, be alert against treachery.

A Short List of Birds & Their Omens:

Blackbird: Blessings will soon fall upon you.

Bluebird: You'll enter a time of happiness.

Cock:
- If a female hears a cock while thinking of her lover, it is a sign of good luck in her relationship with him.
- If a bride or groom hears a cock crowing on the wedding day, there may be trouble in the marriage.
- To see a white cock is a sign of good luck.
- If a cock crows facing the front door of house, it is predicting the arrival of a stranger.
- Wether omen - *"If the cock goes crowing to bed he will wake up with a wet head"*

Corncrake: This is a warning of misfortune to come.

Crane: Peace. An argument will soon come to rest.

Crow: Divine law and detailed messengers. This bird is

often mistakenly held to be of evil portent. More than one crow seen on your left are a sign of misfortune. An uneven number of calls means bad weather and even means good weather- see section on "The Language of the Crows."

Cuckoo:
- *"The cuckoo is a merry bird who brings good tidings." It is the* messenger of Thor, so to hear or see a cuckoo is considered generally good luck and brings a gift or either marriage blessings, health or strength.
- A child born on the day when the first cuckoo is heard will be very lucky
- To hear the call of a cuckoo on the right, turn your money over and wish, It is an omen of upcoming prosperity. Nevertheless if the bird is heard on the left the power of the omen is lessened or can indicate adultery. *"The cuckoo then on every tree mocks married men."*
- However it is not good luck to her the bird before you eat.

Curlew: There is an impending storm.

Dove: Bringer of peace and happiness
- A most favorable omen for lovers.
- Luck in love and a time of peace and wealth.
- However, coal miners believe that a dove flying around the pit-head is bad luck.

Duck: Generally good luck and prosperity.
- If you hear a duck quacking, expect prosperity soon.
- To see this bird fly is a great sign for those who are in trouble, it signifies hope.

Eagle: This bird is a good sign. You are protected by the gods. To see an eagle is to be touched by God.

Flamingo: Lies will become known; you will become aware of a betrayal.

Goose: Faithfulness, communication, and travel.
Eating goose from the equinox to September 29th
will make you never want for money all year round. Scrying is done using the breast bone of the Goose eaten at this time. Allow the bone to dry out and crack or hold it over a fire till it cracks. then you can scry the symbols using the symbols in this book.

Gull: Do not worry about any of the situations around you. You will adapt easily. Don't squabble.

Hawk: (aegithus) Look beyond your current problems.
- The observer should be on his/her guard against enemies who are stronger and more powerful than him/her.
- There are deeper issues not being discussed that will bring peace once confronted.
- To see one at weddings or the beginning of agriculture is unfavorable.

Hen: Predictors of weather.
- If they go out during the rain it will last most of the day.
- If they run for shelter, it will be a short rain.
- If they gather on an hill and clean themselves, rain is coming.
- To hear a hen crowing means personal illness.
- If a hen comes into the home of a newly married couple and cackles the woman will dominate the marriage.

Hummingbird: A wish will come true or a miracle will happen.

Lark: A time of happiness is coming. You will feel content in all things.

Loon: You will spend some extra time alone. This is not a negative sign but rather a positive one as it is causing you to be introspective about your path and place in life.

Magpie:
- To hear a magpie warble means guests are coming.
- A magpie purchased on the roof of a house shows stability.
- To see one magpie upon the left presages death or sadness. If you see one magpie by itself turn around 3 times and make a cross on the ground with your shoe and spit into the direction of the bird to ward off any ills. To meet two or more of these birds however is a good sign. One–bad luck. Two–good luck. Three–marriage. Four–a birth. The omen varies with the number of magpies encountered, according to this famous rhyme concerning these birds:

One for sorrow, two for joy,
Three for a girl, for for a boy,
Five for silver, six for gold,
Seven for a secret, never to be told,
Eight for a wish, nine for a kiss,
Ten for a time of joyous bliss.

This rhyme is also applied to counting sneezes.

Owl: Wisdom or warning.
- You will soon gain a kernel of wisdom or spiritual insight.
- Loss of virginity
- If an owl continues to hoots during the day or outside of your home, it can mean illness. Knot you handkerchief and throw some salt into the fire to ward off bad luck.
- Hooting tells of good weather to come.

- See the section on "The Language of the Owl"

Parrot: Warns you not to try to mimic your friends or be ostentatious, but speak your mind.

Peacock:
- Beware of your pride and vanity. They may get in the way of making connections or healing a situation.
- Some people falsely think peacock feathers are bad luck and will not have them in their home. They are only bad luck for unfaithful men. Some women use them to test their husband's faithfulness. If he has a run of bad luck he has questions to answer.
- Therefor peacock feathers are bad luck in the theatre.
- The peacock is a guardian and its call tells you to be on your guard.

Pelican: Pay close attention to people around you. There may be trouble brewing.

Pheasant: You are approaching a time when you will feel very positive and confident.

Raven:
King Arthur was believed to have been transformed into a raven by his sister after he died. so it is unlucky to s
If you see one traveling to the north, it means you will feel a connection to an ancestor or loved one on the other side.
If it travels to the east, you will soon hear news.
If it travels to the west, you will take part in an emotionally fulfilling situation.
If it flies to the south, beware of your passion, as it will soon burn out.

Robin: Bringer of good luck and good weather.
- Cheerful song - good weather
- Sad song bad weather

- Bad luck to kill one
- Bad luck to touch its eggs

Rook: Good luck is yours.
- If it abandons it nest or the nest is destroyed that portends misfortune
- Flying high - good weather
- Flying low - bad weather

Rooster: You will be proud of an upcoming situation.

Seagull: Seafarers believe that seagulls are the spirit of dead sailors that will not land on the ship where they died. To this day seagulls will avoid ships that have experienced heavy loss of human life. Therefore it is bad luck to kill them. Also unlucky to kill them for practical reasons, as they scavenge and keep the foreshore clean.

Sparrow: Psychopompus - see the section on "Sparrows as Death Omens."
- If you are in love, then your connection with your partner will grow stronger.
- If you aren't in a relationship, you will have luck finding your partner or soulmate.

Stork: Fertility symbol. According to German folklore, if it perches on your house, you will have good luck, peace and happiness for the next year.

Swallow: Good fortune overall.
- If a swallow or a martin builds a nest in the eves of your home it is very good luck.
- If the nest is abandoned or destroyed then it is bad luck for the home.
- If you are on the water, then land is near.

Swan: You will come into a situation that you will handle with finesse and grace.

- Good luck if seen at sea. This is rare as they do not go far out to sea.
- Seeing a swan means ghosts near by.
- Orpheus, the greatest bard in mythology, was changed into a swan after his death and therefore it is said that swans can predict their own death with their swan song.

Turkey: A sign that you will soon give something precious away.

Vulture: Money trouble and disruptions in life.

Wagtail: Good luck.

Woodpecker: You are protected.
- Carrying a woodpecker beak is believed to protect you form bee and wasp stings.
- If the woodpecker calls loudly then thunder and lightning are on the way.

Wren: Sacred bird of Scryers, Psychics and Soothsayers. Sacred to Druids.
- Bringer of good luck.
- However, if you kill or harm one you will break a bone.

Various versions of **"The Bird Counting Rhyme"** exist, but here are the basics:

- **One**: Sorrow. An unhappy event. A change for the worse. Maybe loss or a death.

- **Two:** Joy. A surprise. A change for the better. Sometimes the finding of something.

- **Three**: Marriage. A celebration. Sometimes the birth of a female child. Other times some significant event around a daughter.
- **Four:** Birth. Usually the birth of a male child. Sometimes a significant event surrounding a son.
- **Five:** Silver. Sometimes costly. Usually a positive transaction.
- **Six**: Gold. Wealth. Sometimes money. Maybe greed. Occasionally a negative transaction.
- **Seven:** Something of spiritual significance. Often a secret. In some cases witchcraft, or the performing of sacred rites.
- **Eight**: Something profound. Death, dying, or a glimpse of Heaven. A life-altering journey or experience.
- **Nine**: Something sensual. Passion, or forbidden delight. In some versions this is corruption, in others it is closer to temptation.
- **Ten:** Something extreme. An overwhelming sensation. Something paid in full.
- **Eleven**: Uncertainty. Waiting. Wanting. May be in relation to a spiritual matter.
- **Twelve**: Fulfillment. Riches (though not always of a material sort). A fruitful labor. Something completed. An end to a problem, or the answer to a question.

You can also use these number allocations to count sneezes and adjudge the meanings of other divinations

Other Bird Oracles

The Egg White Oracle

Birds and all things to do with birds have been used as an oracle since the dawn of time.

This egg white method became popular with common folk in Europe in the 16-1700's after it became against the law to go to your local witch for help.

Method:
- Take a fresh egg, separate the white from the yolk.
- Pour the white into a bowl or a cup that has been filled with water.
- Leave the container uncovered.
- After a day, the white of the egg will have formed into clots.
- One or more of these clots will form a recognizable symbol.
- Use our symbol guide at the end of this book to help you interpret what this can mean for you or your client.

Chicken Scrying:

This is a funny easily done traditional household method of Augury that was used in ancient Greece and Rome. It might be comical but hey, their cultures have been very successful so maybe there was something to it.

Method:
- Throw chicken feed onto the ground in front of the chicken coop. Then open the coop.
- If the chicken leap out of the pen hungrily and eat it is good and a favorable response to your question.
- The greedier they are the better. If they drop food from trying to get too much and from pecking so hard it is a big "yes" and portended success and happiness.
- If the chickens did not immediately run to eat or scattered the food with their wings, flew away or didn't even notice the food, it was considered a "no" or a bad omen.

Sparrows - As Death Omens

It is considered bad luck to catch a sparrow and keep it as they convey souls to the after-life and you may trap a soul along with it. Consequently, an old Norwegian omen developed that when a death is about to occur a sparrow will deliver the message to you, via eye contact. When the sparrow does this, it is not just some random bird flying past casually glancing at you. The sparrow will peck at the window to get your attention; it will behave in a manner not natural to a wild animal. The bird will look you in the eyes; it will do whatever it takes to get your attention and hold it for a very long moment, then fly off.

This sounds like a silly superstition, but many claim that every time a sparrow tries very hard to get a person's attention, within two weeks someone close to them dies. here are some accounts:

A mature woman and her mother were on the patio as a sparrow flew up and fluttered in front of the older woman's face. The younger woman was surprised as her mother began to cry saying, "I don't want to lose anyone right now." The younger woman scolded her mother and told her to stop being so superstitious, Yet their grandmother died two weeks later.

"When I was in my early 20s, my boyfriend and I were cleaning his father's basement. They had a broken window down there and they had just put some heavy plastic over the window until they could replace it. As we were cleaning, my boyfriend said, "What is with this crazy bird?"

I looked over and he was standing in front of the broken window and here was a sparrow in the window well, pecking at the plastic. My boyfriend poked the plastic back and the bird started poking more frantically. I yelled, "Get away from it!" He then slapped the plastic with his hand and the sparrow stood there in the window well and just stared at him and then after a long while flew away.

He said, "That was one fearless bird."

I told him, "Someone is going to die. That's an omen."

He laughed at me, but one and a half weeks later his uncle passed away."

Anonymous Contributor

The Language of Ravens and Crows

Crow are not the omens of death as portrayed on Poe novels and hollywood movies. They are messengers. There is a language and meaning in the behavior of ravens and crows, which accurately convey messages and portents to those sensitive souls who are receptive to them. These can be interpreted and understood, if observed correctly. The more attention you give to the actions of ravens and crows, the more apt they will be to respond to your interest. If you keep a compass and this guide handy and you can quickly develop a new and rewarding relationship with these intelligent and helpful creatures.

Four Types of Ravens & Crows & What They Mean
There are Brahmin, Kshatriya, Vaishya and Sudra ravens and crows:-
- *Albino*, piebald (Kurrajongs) or light with white or blue eyes *Brahmins*; Rare and are very good luck;

- Those with *red eyes*
    Kshatriyas; Warriors, bringing strength, warning, defence or strife

- Those with *stocky bodies with yellow or black eyes*
    Vaishyas; Neutral

- Those with *lean bodies,* refusing to eat meat
    Sudras. Brining bad news, lack and loss

Next, you should be aware of the different sound of the bird cries that the ravens and crows are making and where you are when they are calling to you.

Interpretations of Raven's Language
- Ka ka (high pitched)   you will obtain something valuable.

- Nga nga (very low pitched) you will encounter suffering.

- Ka kha (high pitched)   you will find some clothes.

- Cha gha (heavy)   your desires will be fulfilled.

- Cha ga   you will obtain some wealth.

These calls will mean different things if you are at home, or traveling. When you are at home, the location of the cawing of the raven or crow should be noted relative to the location of your dwelling as well as what part of the house you are in. For example if you hear a raven or a crow calling when you are at your altar or whist in meditation, it relates to spiritual issues; at your work desk; financial or business matters are portended, or whilst in the living room means that they are bringing you news about your home life. If you are outdoors, the interpretation is covered in the section on traveling.

Thirdly You should also note what period of the day contact occurs. This is done by dividing the daylight hours roughly into five sections.

First Period (First light - sunrise - early morning)

When a raven or crow caws in the:
- East   your wishes and prayers will come true.
- Southeast   an enemy will come.
- South   friends will come.
- Southwest   you will achieve some unexpected gains.
- West   a strong wind.
- Northwest   a guest is coming.
- North   lost property will be found.
- Northeast   a female guest is coming.
- Overhead   a guest coming.

Second Period (Mid-morning until mid-day)
When a raven caws in the:
- East   a close friend or relative is coming.
- South   praise or a rise in status.
- Southwest   family lineage will increase.
- West   a long distance journey.
- Northwest   the ruler/government is to be replaced.
- North   great fortune.

- Northeast   a quarrel will occur.

- Overhead   earnest desires fulfilled.

Third Period (early afternoon until mid afternoon)
When a raven or crow caws in the:
- East   you will find something valuable.

- Southeast   a fight or argument will occur.

- South   a wind rising.

- Southwest   an enemy arriving.

- West   a female arriving.

- Northwest   a close friend or relative coming.

- North   a good friend or sweetheart will arrive.

- Northeast   something will burn.

- Overhead   favour with authority or government officials.

Fourth Period (later afternoon)
When a raven or crow caws in the:
- East   unpleasant events to occur.

- South   guests arriving.

- Southeast   you will acquire something valuable.

- Southwest   strong wind coming.

- West   a storm coming.

- Northwest   finding lost property.

- North   Authority figure coming.

- Northeast   a raise in status and position.

- Overhead   hunger or famine.

Fifth Period (sunset until dark)
When a raven caws in the:
- East   arrival of an enemy.

- Southeast   you will suffer a loss.

- South   death from disease will occur.

- Southwest   desires fulfilled.

- Northwest   you will come into some wealth.

- West   a friend or relative coming.

- North   a governmental official will receive an honour.

- Overhead   you will attain what you have in mind.

Signs Whilst Travelling
When travelling near dams, rivers and other things connected with water, as well as along gorges, and at

crossroads, a raven cawing on the right side means the journey will be successful.

When travelling or walking on the road, a raven cawing from behind means things sought after will surely be acquired.

If it is:

- flapping its wings - great obstacles will be encountered;

- catches your hair with its beak - a sign of death;

- eating refuse or filth - food and drink will be obtained;

- cawing from a thorny bush - an enemy will attack you;

- cawing from a dead tree - there will be no food or water;

- cawing and sitting on a castle or manor house - good lodging will be found;

- cawing from a place on your mat - the arrival of an enemy is predicted;

- facing a door - a great danger is predicted;

- holding cloth in its beak - garments will be found;

- cawing from your forehead - it is a sign of death;

- cawing from a roof with a red thread in its beak - the house will be burnt;

- holding a twig in its beak - something will be found;

- cawing at sunrise - you will find something valuable;
- just cawing - your desires will be fulfilled.

- If many ravens gather and caw early in the morning - it is predicted that a strong wind will blow.

Nest Location Interpretations
Another thing you should pay special attention to is the location of nests you happen to see.
If raven makes its nest:
- on the east face of a tree - a very prosperous year with abundant rainfall;

- on the southern side of a tree - agriculture will be bad;

- on the middle of a tree truck - great danger is predicted;

- below the half mark of a tree - attack and defeat by an enemy is predicted;

- in a wall, or ground or by the water side - some misfortune will fall on the government.

Warding off Misfortune
If you observe indications of danger or misfortune from the crows and ravens, you must offer the ravens and the crows some torma to help ward off misfortune. Torma is Tibetan cone shaped cakes usually made from flour and water, but sometimes flour and meat. The favorite dish of the ravens and crows is a torma made out of a frog's flesh, or cane-toad if you are in Queensland! The crows and ravens are indeed warding off the misfortune to this

country from this plague of feral pests. The crows and ravens have proved to be the only natural enemies of the introduced cane-toad. They are smart enough to flip these creatures on to their poisonous backs and eat them stomach first leaving the toxic skin behind.

Putting It Together
As with any new language, it takes practice. You have to learn to combine the many parts of speech and actions peculiar to that race, to get an accurate understanding of what is trying to be expressed to you. In the language of the crows and ravens, you must combine the above elements to grasp the basic messages. For example:- If you hear a high pitched caw coming from a plumpish looking crow or a raven behind you as you walk down the street it is a good sign. Observing other details will tell you what good news it is trying to bring you. If this occurs whilst you are walking to work about 8.30-10.00 am then it is probably good news about a pay rise or a promotion. If you observe a lot of crows or ravens together at sunrise cawing happily in a tree or on some wires, it means the wind will pick up later in the day, no matter what the weather man has predicted. I hope you have as much fun learning this new language as I did from my teacher! You will find once you start listening to the crows and ravens a special one will befriend you. You will see it often and it will become your personal familiar, bringing you valuable news and warnings.

So next time you cross paths with a raven, don't think "Stone the crows!" Instead, ask what these 'Messengers of the Goddess' are trying to tell us, if we are smart enough to take the time to listen.

© Copyright Rev. Dr. S. D'Montford Thursday, 14 September 2006. Sydney Australia
Reference: - "Folk Culture of Tibet" by Norbu Chophel

The Owl

A wise old owl lived in an oak;
The more she saw the less she spoke;
The less she spoke the more she heard:
Why can't we be more like that wise old bird?
                                        Edward Hersey Richards

The owl, the totem of wisdom, has long been associated with the craft of the wise. It is not an accident that the word knOWLedge contains the word owl. Pop culture has linked the owl with witches, wizards, and magicians from Disney cartoons to Catweasel and of currently reaching celebrity status with Hedwig from the Harry Potter series.

Silent mysterious and ever watchful, the revered image of the owl appears in the most unlikely places. There is even a tiny depiction of an owl in the corner of the US one dollar bill. This is a nod to the image of the owl on the coin that was the most widely used in history, the ôï ôåôñáäñá-ìï, the four drachmas, which has the picture of Goddess Athena on its reverse side

Capital cities such as Canberra and Washington DC have the out line of an owl in their road system. Why is this? It is the symbol of Athena the Goddess of wisdom and the patron of the city Athens. Our system of western government, commerce, and education are modeled upon Athens. Therefore, it is understandable that our modern designers and town planners would acknowledge such an illustrious patron.

Why Was The Owl Sacred To Athena?

Athena was the child of Zeus and Métis the Goddess of thinking. Zeus himself gave birth to his daughter. She sprang out from the head of her father fully mature and dressed in armor. She quickly became her father's favorite child. She was clever and useful to him. She protected and aided her fathers other illegitimate human sons to become heroes even lending them the wisdom of her owl on occasions. She fell in love with Odysseus for his cunning and clever mind yet was too intelligent to consummate such an uneven relationship. She remained pure thought, symbolically a virgin, and she completely avoided sexual liaisons with any of the other Gods.

Athena won the patronage and the right to have her main shrine in the city of Athens, which was later named for her, by conjuring up an olive tree on the Acropolis. This divine gift was judged by the people to be so useful that they immediately handed patronage to her and built the Parthenon, as her temple.

The ancient Greeks used to attribute the epithet "Parthenon" meaning "The Virgin" to the Goddess because she represented the purity of both the body and the mind and they also called her Ãëáõî -The Shining One – from which we get the word Athena. The same name was used by them for the owl- ãëáõî and both the Goddess as well as the bird were considered "The Wise One." However, the owl was more than a symbol of Athena. In myth, she was a shape shifter, sometimes appearing as an owl. To the ancients Athena = Owl. Only rarely does she appear with a symbol of an owl and she never appears in the myths with an owl.

How Did Athena Come To Possess Her Owl?
Nyctimene, daughter of Epopeus, king of the island of Lesbos, is said to have been a beautiful and intelligent girl. Her father, smitten by passion, raped her. Overcome by shame, she hid herself in the woods and would not come out nor would she speak. Athena out of pity changed her into an owl. Still suffering from shame, the owl to this day will not come into the light but appears only at night. Because of this myth, the owl was often the symbol of old spinsters or lesbians.

This is similar to the story of the Goddess Bloddewed in Welsh mythology. She was a supernatural beauty, a woman created from flowers. Unfortunately, she fell in love with another man, rather than the man she was created to marry. She was cursed by her husband's uncle, turning her into an owl. "You are never to show your face to the light of day, rather you shall fear other birds; they will be hostile to you, and it will be their nature to maul and molest you wherever they find you."

The Wise Old Owl and Aesop
Aesop's fables often had wise old owls to which other animals would go to for advice. In one of his fables, the owl in her wisdom, counsels all the other birds that when the acorn first began to sprout, to pull it up out of the ground and not allow it to grow. She said the tree from the acorns would nourish mistletoe, from which an irremediable poison for birds (bird lime) would be extracted and by which they would be captured. The owl next advised them to pluck up the seed of the flax, which men had sown, so that men could not weave linen from it and therefore could not cloth themselves and would go away. When the other birds laughed and asked why they

would want men to go away, the owl pointed out an archer approaching. She predicted that this man despite being on foot, would contrive darts aided with feathers, which would fly faster than the wings of the birds themselves. The birds gave no credence to these warning words, but considered the owl mad. After, finding her words were true, they were amazed at her knOWLedge and deemed her the wisest of birds. Yet no matter how much they beseeched her, she never again gave them advice, but kept her secrets silently to herself. Therefore, an appearance of an owl in your yard at night is often taken as a silent warning to do commonsense things to prevent a calamity.

Owl Lore From Other Parts Of The World
In Australia, owls are sacred. Owls cannot be eaten because, "...your sister is an owl - and the owl is your sister!" Aborigines believe bats represent the souls of men and owls the souls of women. This belief of owls being departed women and bats departed men appears in many other cultures.

In the USA, owls represent old people and should be respected. Louisiana Cajuns believe that you should get up from bed and turn your left shoe upside down to avert disaster, if you hear an owl calling late at night. However, you must never kill an owl or revenge will be visited upon your family.

In Wales, an owl heard hooting in a built up area means an unmarried girl has lost her virginity. If a woman is pregnant and she alone hears an owl hoot outside her house at night then her child will be blessed. The French also believe that when a pregnant woman hears an owl it is an omen that her child will be a girl. The Wend people say that the sight of an owl makes childbirth easier. Yet, in Germany if an owl hoots as a child is born, the infant will have an unhappy life.

In Transylvania, farmers scare away owls by walking round their fields naked (or so they tell us!)

The Tungus/Tartar tribes on the Alti-Himalayan region, from Siberia to Mongolia universally consider the owl to be a good omen. It is from them that we get the English word shaman, and their shaman believed that they could assume the form of an owl. The hunters carry owl claws so that, if they are killed, their souls can use them to climb up to heaven. They consider the owl to be sacred because one once saved the life of Genghis Khan. In Afghanistan, the owl gave man flint and iron to make fire. In exchange, man gave the owl his feathers. Up as far as Greenland the Inuit see the owl as a source of guidance and help. In addition, across to the Bantu of Central Africa, there the owl is the familiar of wizards.

In China, the owl is associated with lightning, because its big eyes brighten the night. They believe that placing owl effigies in each corner of a home will protect it against lightning. The deep sound of the flap of its wings and the deep hoot that break the evening stillness, have earned it an association with drums. To them the owl is a symbol of yang, positive, masculine, bright, active, energy.

The Ainu people of Japan believe that the Eagle Owl is a messenger of the gods and a divine ancestor. They drink a toast to the Eagle Owl before hunting. They nail images of owls to their houses to ensure plenty of food for their family in the lean times. However, to them, the Screech Owl warns against danger and the Barn Owl and Horned Owl are demonic.

Also In Arabia, the Screech Owl and the Horned Owl are birds of ill omen, in the form of Lilith, their Goddess of death, who carries off children at night. To them owls also represent the souls of people who have died unavenged. According to an ancient Arabic treatise, from each female owl comes two eggs. One egg has the power to cause hair to fall out and one held the power to restore it.

The Rastafarians in Jamaica have an easy way to ward off any bad luck from owls. When they see an owl they call out: "Salt and pepper for your mammy."

The ceramic blue Evil Eyes often worn to protect people from evil are representations of owls eyes. Once real owls eyes were worn but it was considered bad luck to kill an owl. The Sympathetic magickal substitution of the ceramic eyes seems to work just fine!

Interpreting The Language Of The Owls

- One hoot was an ill omen
- Two meant success in anything that would be started soon after
- Three represented a woman being married into the family
- Four indicated a disturbance
- Five denoted coming travel

- Six meant guests were on the way

- Seven was a sign of mental distress

- Eight foretold sudden death

- And nine symbolised good fortune

When you want to travel, listen to the owls. Owls make two different sounds, a hoot, and a screech. The first means it is safe to go, and the second means it is better to stay at home.

Owl Wisdom/Memory Spell

You will need: -
- Yellow household candle

- Owl talisman

- A piece of yellow cord or fine ribbon

- A teaspoon of honey and

- A teaspoon of olive oil

Choose from one or a combination of these oils or incenses appropriate to what you want to achieve
- Honeysuckle -to pass a test,
- Lilac - to relieve nervousness,
- Bramhi -improve memory and focus
- Cinnamon - for wisdom and cleverness

Then: -
- Ring a bell 3 times

- Carve your name or name of a person you are aiding, into the candle and anoint with the olive oil.

- Light your incense and then your candle.

- Press the talisman to your forehead then tie it to yourself

- Swallow the honey slowly. Let it trickle down your throat. Visualise it clearing your mind and strengthening your intellect.

- Then while standing before your altar chant: -

"Oh, mighty Athena, bright eyed and cleaver
Help me now with my ernest endeavor.
Grant me clarity and wisdom now I pray
That throughout my studies (or test or whatever you need to focus on), *my mind will not stray.*
Keep it receptive, open, and clear for me.
As I do will, so mote it be!"

Don't remove the talisman until after you have done what you needed to do.

©Copyright Rev. Dr. S. D'Montford. Thursday, July 26, 2007. Gold Coast. Australia.

Ogham
The Secret Language of Trees

Trees can spell-out messages for us if we know how to read their language. The Ogams is their alphabet of 25 markings or symbols that were also connected to sacred trees of the Celtic druids. They represent the branches on the trees and are read from the ground up, fortunately for us groundlings. So by identifying these symbols as you walk pas trees or through a forrest you can receive messages.

The Ogham script is Old Irish text dating between the 3rd and the 6th century. Ogham inscriptions are found exclusively in Ireland, Scotland, and Wales. The Ogham letters are divided into four groups, each containing five letters. This yields a total of 20 Ogham letters.

When inscribed on stones, Oghams are written vertically from bottom to top. The following chart lists all Ogham letters in their vertical forms, along with their Old Irish

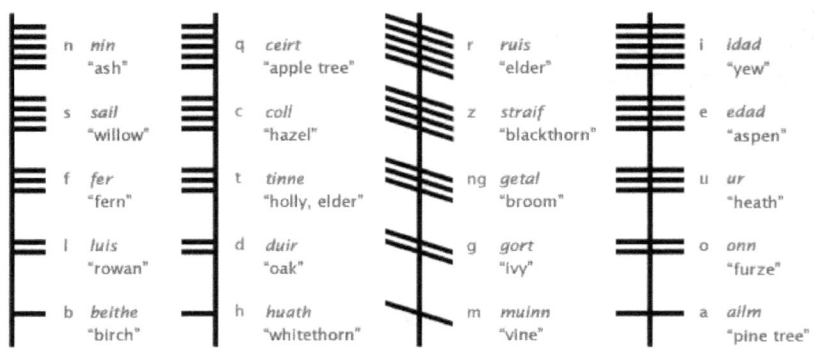

n	*nin* "ash"	q	*ceirt* "apple tree"	r	*ruis* "elder"	i	*idad* "yew"		
s	*sail* "willow"	c	*coll* "hazel"	z	*straif* "blackthorn"	e	*edad* "aspen"		
f	*fer* "fern"	t	*tinne* "holly, elder"	ng	*getal* "broom"	u	*ur* "heath"		
l	*luis* "rowan"	d	*duir* "oak"	g	*gort* "ivy"	o	*onn* "furze"		
b	*beithe* "birch"	h	*huath* "whitethorn"	m	*muinn* "vine"	a	*ailm* "pine tree"		

names and meanings.

Sometimes the vowels use dots rather than lines intersecting the vertical axis.

In some cases, mostly in manuscripts, Ogham is written horizontally from right to left.

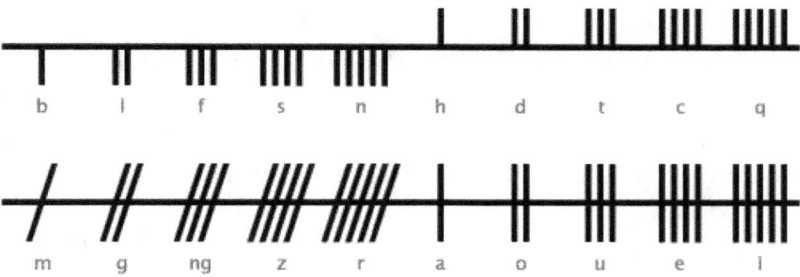

A fifth group of letters called forfeda is also listed.

Ogham diagrams contributed by Lawrence K Lo http://www.ancientscripts.com/ogham.html

You can carve these onto wood for divination purposes. This is known as casting the ogham staves

The word Ogham comes from "Ogmios" the Celtic deity of eloquence. He looked like an older version of Heracles with equivalent attributes. He was worshipped by the Gauls, the Celtic people of France. He was the creator of the ogham alphabet around 300AD. Ogmios, "the personification of speech," and equates the Irish Ogma, inventor of writing. The Romans associated him with Hermes and Mercury whose attributes are again found in the Norse Woden, Odysseus, the Logos and in the Hindu god Indra.

He is pictured as an older man with wrinkled and sunburnt skin who was dynamic and strong. Yet, he had accomplished his feats through glorious speech rather than thuggery. His speech shows itself best in his old age. He draws a multitude of joyful followers and admirers by beautiful chains of gold and amber attached to their ears. The other end of the chains are fixed to his tongue, and he bestows on his captives a

smiling face. The chains indicate the bond between the orator's tongue and the ears of enraptured listeners. His sacred instrument was the bull roarer, also the sacred instrument of Dionysian Mysteries. The bull roarer was ritually used the world over for evoking primal cosmic resonances capable of activating the bindu seed of creation.

Nostradamus prophesied that the "Great Genius Ogmios" or a new form of writing, is the counterforce to the Antichrist who will help tear down the tyranny and balance the universe in a way that is harmonious to man's central spiritual source. The "glory of the sun" is behind Ogmios; he is a man of great stature, but has a direct, sometimes gruff personality. He makes a good friend but a terrible enemy. Likewise, the Ogam scrying is a useful and powerful ally.

Ogam Staves Scrying

Oghams can be used as a form of earth scrying. Only seven of the original secret symbols are used for scrying. If you so choose to make your own ogham sticks, try to make the symbols on their correlating sacred timber from their sacred trees. (Please see the symbol guide on the previous pages.)

These are:-
Birch: B; Sunday; rebirth and purification.

Willow: S; Monday; represents intuition, listening to your inner voice and wisdom.

Holly: T; Tuesday; the Waning year; domestic security and concerns.

Hazel: C; Wednesday; official wisdom, justice and following the law.

Oak: D; Thursday; the Waxing year - from winter to summer solstice.

Apple: Q; Friday; fertility and immortality.

Elder: R; Saturday; security, firm foundations and a bridge between two lives.

Quick Method:
After having written these 7 out - on staves or just pieces of paper - hold a question in your mind and draw one out to see your quick message. Learning to read the full alphabet from trees themselves, gives you a much deeper answer.

Runes
The Stones, That Spell Out the Future

Runes are the letters in a set of related alphabets from the Germanic languages known as runic alphabets. Runes predate the Oghams by only 100 years and was still a living written language during the reign of Queen Elisabeth 1st of England in the early 1600s.

Runes were used to write before the adoption of the Latin alphabet. Other variants are also known through out Scandinavian called futhark or fuþark (derived from their first six letters of the alphabet: F, U, Þ, A, R, and K) Elder Furthark is the most commonly used alphabet for divination

Rune Stones are used as a system of divination, and decision making. Indeed Runes are thought by some to be a way of interacting with both the spirit and the living world. Thus the word "Rune" means "whisper" or "secret".

The myths of the origins of the Runes is attributed to the Norse king of the gods Odin. After hanging upside down on the World Tree "Ysgadril" for nine days he reached the same realization as the reader of this book and he "saw" how the magical and systematic power of signs related to the world around him. He invented the Runes to represent this system.

There are many similarities between The Ogmios the inventor of the Oghams and Odin the inventor of the Runes

Runes Casting Method:

- Write these symbols, given on the following pages, on to small flat stones.

- Keep them in a leather pouch.

- When an answer to a question is required the Runes are shaken in their bag to wake them up.

- Reach into the rune bag, stir them around with your hand and pick up a handful.

- Then "cast" them. Runes are ideally cast facing the sun onto a white cloth.

- After casting the stones onto the cloth some will be face down. Ignore them. The ones which have fallen the right side up are read.

- Take a note of which ones are face up but reversed or upside down. Reversed Runes have a different meaning and can affect the reading as a whole. Some runes look the same upside down and right side up. These cannot be "reversed." Nevertheless, any of the runes may appear as a "merkstave" or dark, if it is covering another rune. Runes that are touching, at right angles to, or covering other runes can be closely working together in some way. Note that a "reversed" or "merkstave" meaning is not the opposite of its primary meaning and is not always a negative connotation. For instance "Perthro" ☒ merkstave can indicate infertility. it can be a very good thing for a woman to find out that she is not pregnant or not very fertile at the moment.

- You have to adjudge the meaning of your answer from all of the Runes that have come out in your cast together to see what they are spelling out for you.
- Look up the meanings here.

Below is a table containing a full set of 24 rune symbols, placed within their Aett or set. The Runic signs are arranged into 3 groups of 8 runes each. These groups

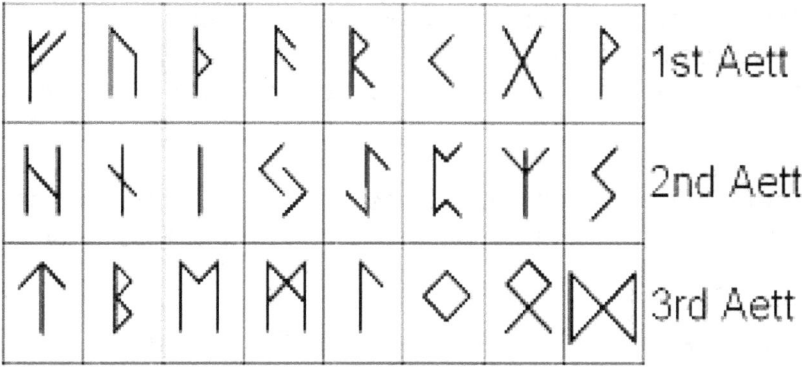

The Elder Futhark

are called Aett (singular) or Aettir (plural) Each Aett is ruled over by a particular Norse God.
:Respectively these entities are:-
- 1st - Freya & Frey - Goddess of fertility and increase
- 2nd - Heindall - The watcher. Keeper of the Rainbow Bridge to the Heavens
- 3rd - Tyr - War leader and spirit of the just

Lawrence K Lo from www.ancientscripts.com has this to say about the aetts: *"What is interesting about these two numbers associated with every rune is that they can be used to write an alternate, "encoded", version of the rune. An encoded rune consists of a central vertical line, with short horizontal lines left of the vertical line determined by the rune's ætt number, and short horizontal lines on the right side determined by the rune's position within its ætt, as illustrated below":*

f u th a r k g w h n i j ae p z s t b e m l ng d o

Some scholars have theorized that this alternate system of representing letters with vertical and horizontal lines has some kind of connection to Ogham, but no solid links have been found yet."

Check to see which aett the majority of the stones in your reading is from. This will show you the theme of your reading.

Freya's Aett - Goddess of fertility and increase

Fehu (F: Domestic cattle, wealth.) Possessions won or earned, earned income, luck. Abundance, financial strength in the present or near future. Sign of hope and plenty, success and happiness. Social success. Energy, foresight, fertility, creation/destruction (becoming). Fehu Reversed or Merkstave: Loss of personal property, esteem, or something that you put in effort to keep. It indicates some sort of failure. Greed, burnout, atrophy, discord. Cowardice, stupidity, dullness, poverty, slavery, bondage.

Uruz: (U: Auroch, a wild ox.) Physical strength and speed, untamed potential. A time of great energy and health. Freedom, energy, action, courage, strength, tenacity, understanding, wisdom. Sudden or unexpected changes (usually for the better). Sexual desire, masculine potency. The shaping of power and pattern, formulation of the self. Uruz Reversed or Merkstave: Weakness, obsession, misdirected force, domination by others. Sickness, inconsistency, ignorance. Lust, brutality, rashness, callousness, violence.

Thurisaz: (TH: Thorn or a Giant.) Reactive force, directed force of destruction and defense, conflict. Instinctual will, vital eroticism, regenerative catalyst. A tendency toward change. Catharsis, purging, cleansing fire. Male sexuality, fertilization. (Thorr, the Thunder god, was of Giant stock.)Thurisaz Reversed or Merkstave: Danger, defenselessness, compulsion, betrayal, dullness. Evil, malice, hatred, torment, spite, lies. A bad man or woman. Rape?

Ansuz: (A: The As, ancestral god, i.e. Odin.) A revealing message or insight, communication. Signals, inspiration, enthusiasm, speech, true vision, power of words and naming. Blessings, the taking of advice. Good health, harmony, truth, wisdom. Ansuz Reversed or Merkstave: Misunderstanding, delusion, manipulation by others, boredom. Vanity and grandiloquence. (Odin is a mighty, but duplicitous god. He always has his own agenda.)

Raidho: (R: Wagon or chariot.) Travel, both in physical terms and those of lifestyle direction. A journey, vacation, relocation, evolution, change of place or setting. Seeing a larger perspective. Seeing the right move for you to make and deciding upon it. Personal rhythm, world rhythm, dance of life. Raidho Reversed or Merkstave: Crisis, rigidity, stasis, injustice, irrationality. Disruption, dislocation, demotion, delusion, possibly a death.

Kenaz: (K: Beacon or torch.) Vision, revelation, knowledge, creativity, inspiration, technical ability. Vital fire of life, harnessed power, fire of transformation and regeneration. Power to create your own reality, the power of light. Open to new strength, energy, and power now. Passion, sexual love. Kenaz Reversed or Merkstave: Disease, breakup, instability, lack of creativity. Nakedness, exposure, loss of illusion and false hope.

Gebo: (G: Gift.) Gifts, both in the sense of sacrifice and of generosity, indicating balance. All matters in relation to exchanges, including contracts, personal relationships and partnerships. Gebo Merkstave (Gebo cannot be reversed, but may lie in opposition): Greed, loneliness, dependence, over-sacrifice. Obligation, toll, privation, bribery.

Wunjo: (W or V: Joy.) Joy, comfort, pleasure. Fellowship, harmony, prosperity. Ecstasy, glory, spiritual reward, but also the possibility of going "over the top". If restrained, the meaning is general success and recognition of worth. Wunjo Reversed or Merkstave: Stultification, sorrow, strife, alienation. Delirium, intoxication, possession by higher forces, impractical enthusiasm. Raging frenzy, berserker.

Heindall's Aett - The watcher and the keeper of the Rainbow Bridge to the Heavens

Hagalaz: (H: Hail.) Wrath of nature, destructive, uncontrolled forces, especially the weather, or within the unconscious. Tempering, testing, trial. Controlled crisis, leading to completion, inner harmony. Hagalaz Merkstave (Hagalaz cannot be reversed, but may lie in opposition): Natural disaster, catastrophe. Stagnation, loss of power. Pain, loss, suffering, hardship, sickness, crisis.

Nauthiz: (N: Need.) Delays, restriction. Resistance leading to strength, innovation, need-fire (self-reliance). Distress, confusion, conflict, and the power of will to overcome them. Endurance, survival, determination. A time to exercise patience. Recognition of one's fate. Major self-initiated change. Face your fears. Nauthiz Reversed or Merkstave: Constraint of freedom, distress, toil, drudgery, laxity. Necessity, extremity, want, deprivation, starvation, need, poverty, emotional hunger.

Isa: (I: Ice.) A challenge or frustration. Psychological blocks to thought or activity, including grievances. Standstill, or a time to turn inward and wait for what is to come, or to seek clarity. This rune reinforces runes around it. Isa Merkstave (Isa cannot be reversed, but may lie in opposition): Ego-mania, dullness, blindness, dissipation. Treachery, illusion, deceit, betrayal, guile, stealth, ambush, plots.

Jera: (J or Y: A year, a good harvest.) The results of earlier efforts are realized. A time of peace and happiness, fruitful season. It can break through

stagnancy. Hopes and expectations of peace and prosperity. The promise of success earned. Life cycle, cyclical pattern of the universe. Everything changes, in its own time. Jera Merkstave (Jera cannot be reversed, but may lie in opposition): Sudden setback, reversals. A major change, repetition, bad timing, poverty, conflict.

Eihwaz: (EI: Yew tree.) Strength, reliability, dependability, trustworthiness. Enlightenment, endurance. Defense, protection. The driving force to acquire, providing motivation and a sense of purpose. Indicates that you have set your sights on a reasonable target and can achieve your goals. An honest man who can be relied upon. Eihwaz Reversed or Merkstave: Confusion, destruction, dissatisfaction, weakness.

Perthro: (P: Lot cup, vagina.) Uncertain meaning, a secret matter, a mystery, hidden things and occult abilities. Initiation, knowledge of one's destiny, knowledge of future matters, determining the future or your path. Pertaining to things feminine, feminine mysteries including female fertility, and vagina. Good lot, fellowship and joy. Evolutionary change. Perthro Reversed or Merkstave: Addiction, stagnation, loneliness, malaise, infertility.

Algiz: (Z or -R: Elk, protection.) Protection, a shield. The protective urge to shelter oneself or others. Defense, warding off of evil, shield, guardian. Connection with the gods, awakening, higher life. It can be used to channel energies appropriately. Follow your instincts. Keep hold of success or maintain a position won or earned. Algiz Reversed: or Merkstave: Hidden danger, consumption by divine forces, loss of divine link. Taboo, warning, turning away, that which repels.

Sowilo: (S: The sun.) Success, goals achieved, honor. The life-force, health. A time when power will be available to you for positive changes in your life, victory, health, and success. Contact between the higher self and the unconscious. Wholeness, power, elemental force, sword of flame, cleansing fire. Sowilo Merkstave (Sowilo cannot be reversed, but may lie in opposition): False goals, bad counsel, false success, gullibility, loss of goals. Destruction, retribution, justice, casting down of vanity. Wrath of god.

Tyr's Aett - War leader and spirit of the just.

Tiwaz: (T: Tyr, the sky god.) Honor, justice, leadership and authority. Analysis, rationality. Knowing where one's true strengths lie. Willingness to self-sacrifice. Victory and success in any competition or in legal matters. Tiwaz Reversed or Merkstave: One's energy and creative flow are blocked. Mental paralysis, over-analysis, over-sacrifice, injustice, imbalance. Strife, war, conflict, failure in competition. Dwindling passion, difficulties in communication, and possibly separation.

Berkano: (B: Berchta, the birch-goddess.) Birth, general fertility, both mental and physical and personal growth, liberation. Regenerative power and light of spring, renewal, promise of new beginnings, new growth. Arousal of desire. A love affair or new birth. The prospering of an enterprise or venture. Berkano Reversed or Merkstave: Family problems and or domestic troubles. Anxiety about someone close to you.

Carelessness, abandon, loss of control. Blurring of consciousness, deceit, sterility, stagnation.

Ehwaz: (E: Horse, two horses.) Transportation. May represent a horse, car, plane, boat or other vehicle. Movement and change for the better. Gradual development and steady progress are indicated. Harmony, teamwork, trust, loyalty. An ideal marriage or partnership. Confirmation beyond doubt the meanings of the runes around it. Ehwaz Reversed or Merkstave: This is not really a negative rune. A change is perhaps craved. Feeling restless or confined in a situation. Reckless haste, disharmony, mistrust, betrayal.

Mannaz: (M: Man, mankind.) The Self; the individual or the human race. Your attitude toward others and their attitudes towards you. Friends and enemies, social order. Intelligence, forethought, create, skill, ability. Divine structure, intelligence, awareness. Expect to receive some sort of aid or cooperation now. Mannaz Reversed or Merkstave: Depression, mortality, blindness, self-delusion. Cunning, slyness, manipulation, craftiness, calculation. Expect no help now.

Laguz: (L: Water, or a leek.) Flow, water, sea, a fertility source, the healing power of renewal. Life energy and organic growth. Imagination and psychic matters. Dreams, fantasies, mysteries, the unknown, the hidden, the deep, the underworld. Success in travel or acquisition, but with the possibility of loss. Laguz Reversed or Merkstave: An indication of a period of confusion in your life. You may be making wrong decisions and poor judgements. Lack of creativity and feelings of being in a rut. Fear, circular motion, avoidance, withering. Madness, obsession, despair, perversity, sickness, suicide.

Ingwaz: (NG: Ing, the earth god.) Male fertility, gestation, internal growth. Common virtues, common sense, simple strengths, family love, caring, human warmth, the home. Rest stage, a time of relief, of no anxiety. A time when all loose strings are tied and you are free to move in a new direction. Listen to yourself. Ingwaz Merkstave (Ingwaz cannot be reversed, but may lie in opposition): Impotence, movement without change. Production, toil, labor, work.

Dagaz: (D: Day or dawn.) Breakthrough, awakening, awareness. Daylight clarity as opposed to nighttime uncertainty. A time to plan or embark upon an enterprise. The power of change directed by your own will, transformation. Hope/happiness, the ideal. Security and certainty. Growth and release. Balance point, the place where opposites meet. Dagaz Merkstave (Dagaz cannot be reversed, but may lie in opposition): A completion, ending, limit, coming full circle. Blindness, hopelessness.

Othala: (O: Ancestral property.) Inherited property or possessions, a house, a home. What is truly important to one. Group order, group prosperity. Land of birth, spiritual heritage, experience and fundamental values. Aid in spiritual and physical journeys. Source of safety, increase and abundance. Othala Reversed or Merkstave: Lack of customary order, totalitarianism, slavery, poverty, homelessness. Bad karma, prejudice, clannishness, provincialism. What a man is bound to.

The Blank Rune: There is no historical support for a "Blank Rune" in runic divination. It was invented in the 1980's. It should not be used in a rune casting. If you bought a rune set with a blank piece, save it in case you lose another rune piece, but don't use it in rune casting.

Rune meanings © by Ingrid Halvorsen. See more on her website "Runes Alphabet of Mystery." http://www.sunnyway.com/runes/meanings.html

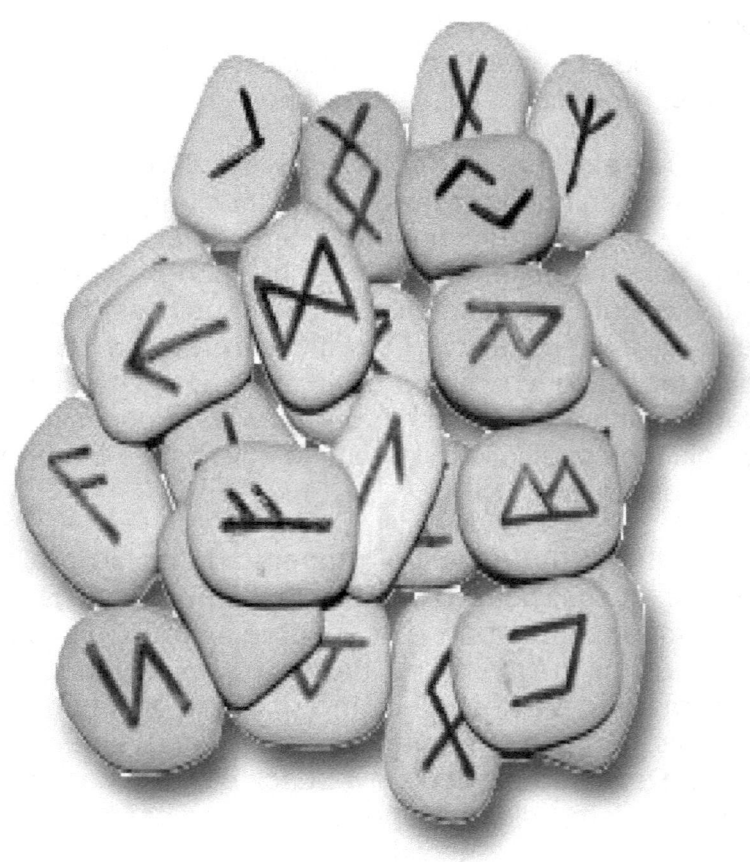

Cartomancy

The art of cartomancy, or divination by playing-cards, dates from the early 1500s. In the museum of Nantes there is a painting, by Van Eyck, representing Philippe le

Bon, Archduke of Austria, and subsequently King of Spain, consulting a fortune-teller by cards. The earliest work on cartomancy was written or compiled by one Francesco Marcolini, and printed at Venice in 1540.

Robert Chambers gave these meaning for the cards in his workThe Book of Days in 1869:-

DIAMONDS
- **King.** A man of very fair complexion; quick to auger, but soon appeased.

- **Queen**. A very fair woman, fond of gaiety, and a coquette.
- **Knave**. A selfish and deceitful relative: fair and false.

- **Ten.** Money. Success in honourable business.

- **Nine.** A roving disposition, combined with honour able and successful adventure in foreign lands.

- **Eight.** A happy prudent marriage, though rather late in life.

- **Seven.** Satire. Scandal. Unpleasant business matters.

- **Six**. Marriage early in life, succeeded by widow-hood.

- **Five.** Unexpected news, generally of a good kind.

- **Four**. An unfaithful friend. A secret betrayed.

- **Trey**. Domestic troubles, quarrels and unhappiness.

- **Deuce.** A clandestine engagement. A card of caution.

- **Ace**. A wedding ring. An offer of marriage.

HEARTS
- **King**. A fair, but not very fair, complexioned man: good natured, but rather obstinate, and, when angered, not easily appeased.

- **Queen.** A woman of the same complexion as the king; faithful, prudent, and affectionate.

- **Knave**. An unselfish relative. A sincere friend. Ten. Health and happiness, with many children. Nine. Wealth. High position in society. The wish-card.

- **Eight**. Fine clothes. Pleasure. Mixing in good society. Going to balls, theatres, & entertainments.

- **Seven.** Many good friends.

- **Six.** Honourable courtship.

- **Five**. A present.

- **Four.** Domestic troubles caused by jealousy.

- **Trey**. Poverty, shame and sorrow, caused by imprudence. A card of caution.

- **Deuce**. Success in life, position in society, and a happy marriage, attained by virtuous discretion.

- **Ace**. The house of the person consulting the decrees of fate.

SPADES
- **King**. A man of very dark complexion, ambitious and unscrupulous.

- **Queen.** A very dark complexioned woman, of malicious disposition. A widow.

- **Knave**. A lawyer. A person to be shunned.

- **Ten**. Disgrace: crime: imprisonment. Death on the scaffold. A card of caution.

- **Nine**. Grief: ruin: sickness: death.

- **Eight**. Great danger from imprudence. A card of caution.

- **Seven**. Unexpected poverty caused by the death of a relative. A lean sorrow.

- **Six**. A child. To the unmarried a card of caution.

- **Five**. Great danger from giving way to bad temper. A card of caution.

- **Four.** Sickness.

- **Trey.** A journey by land. Tears.

- **Deuce**. A removal.

- **Ace**. Death; malice; a duel; a general misfortune.

CLUBS
- **King.** A dark complexioned man, though not so dark as the king of spades: upright, true, and affectionate.

- **Queen.** A woman of the same complexion, agreeable, genteel, and witty.

- **Knave.** A sincere, but rather hasty-tempered friend. Ten. Unexpected wealth, through the death of a relative. A fat sorrow.

- **Nine**. Danger caused by drunkenness. A card of caution.

- **Eight.** Danger from covetousness. A card of caution.

- **Seven**. A prison. Danger arising from the opposite sex. A card of caution.

- **Six**. Competence by hard-working industry.

- **Five.** A happy, though not wealthy marriage.

- **Four**. Danger of misfortunes caused by inconstancy, or capricious temper. A card of caution.

- **Trey**. Quarrels. Or in reference to time may signify three years, three mouths, three weeks, or three days. it also denotes that a person will be married more than once.

- **Deuce**. Vexation, disappointment.

- **Ace**. A letter

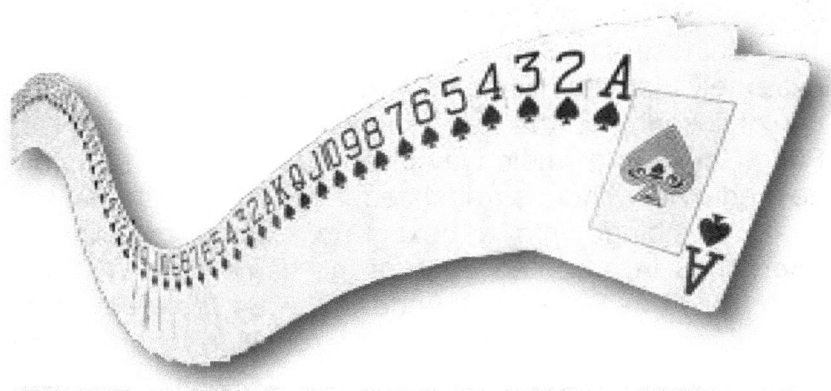

Geomancy

Geomancy is a form of earth divination. It is a complex art of interpretation and skill in recognizing patterns - it is not about just looking up predefined answers. This method interprets the random patterns formed by tossed handfuls of natural objects, shells, bones, stones etc. or random man-made dots and lines. Sixteen figures formed by this randomized process are interpreted.

This may be the oldest oracle method, originating as a basic form of shamanic divination in sub-Saharan Africa, where grids and dots are drawn in the dirt. Yet, philosophers, occultists, and theologians in Europe wrote detail treaties on this subject until the 17th century. It may have entered the west from the Middle Eastern practice of casting lots. Geomantic figures later became dice. Dice divination or rolling four dice to see potential outcomes can be a shorthand form of this divination. The 1970's popular horror novel "The Dice Man" was based upon dice geomancy. The reference in Hermetic texts to the mythical Ṭumṭum al-Hindi potentially points to an Indian origin.

The Chinese divination practice of the I Ching is an extremely complex form of geomancy that extends via the philosophy of the Tao and the are of placement of Fung Shui into a whole way of living. In brief, a randomly derived binary code is translated into 2 of 8 tri-grams and finally combined into a hexagram, whose meaning is referenced in a sacred book of the same name - The I Ching or "The Book of Changes. The 64, hexagrams of the I-Ching is a smaller set of resulting charts than

The eight trigrams used in I Ching.

geomancy. Yet this way of living is a vastly complex subject that cannot be done justice with a brief mention in a work on other methods. However, it will be a rewarding course of study for the serious divination student.

The field of geomancy is complex yet simple. Its mathematical binary combination systems have been the inspiration for predictive and risk assessment software.

The 16 geomantic figures are the primary symbols used in the art of divinatory geomancy. These were believed to be messages from angels in Islamic culture and that geomancy is a skill from God.

The Geomantic Figures
The 16 geomantic figures are the primary symbols used in the art of divinatory geomancy. Each geomantic figure represents a certain state of the world or the mind, and can be interpreted in various ways based upon the query put forth and the method used to generate the figures.

Via (Way)
- Other names: wayfarer, candle.
- Meanings: change, a journey, alternation between good and ill fortune.

The figure resembles a road or path. It is considered bad with most things, but good with concerns of roads, travels, or journeys. Astrologically it is associated with Cancer and the waning Moon, and its element is water. Via is active, and as such the figure indicates change more than any other figure. It is associated with the deities Diana and Mercury, and the angels Gabriel and Muriel. It is associated with the stomach.

Caput Draconis (Head of the Dragon)
Other names: inner threshold, threshold coming in, upper boundary, high tree, upright staff.
Meaning: beginnings and upward movement; a favorable figure.

The figure resembles the astrological symbol the north node of the Moon. It is neutral figure but fortunate with starting or beginning new things. It is favorable for beginnings and profit, and otherwise favorable with other favorable figures, and unfavorable with unfavorable ones. It is associated with the planets Jupiter and Venus, and assigned to the zodiac sign of Sagittarius; Its element is earth. It is associated with the deities Venus, Jove, and Vulcan, and the angels Sachiel, Anael, and Zuriel. It is associated with the right arm.

Cauda Draconis (Tail of the Dragon)
Other names: outer threshold, threshold going out, lower boundary.
Meaning: endings and downward movement; an unfavorable figure.

The figure of the south node of the Moon. It is considered so very bad in most situations, that if this was the first figure drawn the geomancy reading was stopped. It is only good in circumstances for ending or completing things that are bad for you. Its astrological sign is Virgo. Its element is fire. It is associated with the deities Mars, Saturn and and Athena, and the angels Cassiel, Samael and Malchidael. It is associated with the left arm.

Puella (Girl)

```
  ♦
 ♦ ♦     Other names: clean face.
  ♦      Meaning: beauty and happiness; a pleasant
         figure, but fickle.
```

The figure resembles the vulva or a woman with exaggerated breasts. It is good in most situations, especially with women, beauty, or feminine situations. Astrologically it is associated with Libra and Venus; Its element is water. It represents peace and passivity, which can be either positive or negative depending on the question being answered, though generally positive, requiring to be acted upon instead of it acting on a situation. It is the symbol of feminine sexuality, balancing the energy of Puer. It is associated with the deities Venus and Vulcan, and the angels Anael and Zuriel. It is associated with the kidneys, lower back, buttocks, and skin.

Puer (Boy)

```
  ♦
  ♦      Other names: beardless, yellow, warrior, man.
 ♦ ♦     Meaning: rashness, violence, energy.
  ♦      The figure is a representation of a sword or erect
```

phallus and refers to male energies, primarily aggression and passion, but also war and male sexuality. It is bad in most cases, but good in traditional male endeavors including love and war. Astrologically it is associated with Aries and Mars. Its element is air. It is associated with the deities Mars and Athena, and the angels Samael and Malchidael. It is associated with the head.

Acquisito (Gain)
Other names: inner grasp, inner wealth, a thing picked up.
Meaning: profit and gain in material matters.

The figure resembles two bowls or cups turned upright. It is good in almost all situations, especially for getting and obtaining things. Astrologically it is associated with Sagittarius and Jupiter, Its element is air. For most charts it is a positive figure, except where a loss is desired. It indicates a gain financially, mentally, or in any other form, or something within one's grasp. It is associated with the deities Jove and Diana, and the angels Sachiel and Adnachiel. It is associated with the hips and thighs.

Amissio (Loss)
Other names: outward grasp, a thing evading or lost.
Meaning: loss in material matters.

The figure is of two bowls or cups turned upside-down. Astrologically, it is associated with Taurus and Venus retrograde. Its element is fire. In general, the figure is bad or negative figure for all charts except those for love. Often it represents something outside of one's grasp. It is associated with the goddess Venus, and the angels Anael and Asmodel. It is associated with the neck and throat.

Carcer (Prison)
Other names: constricted, poor old man, lock.
Meaning: restriction, limitation, imprisonment.
The figure is the outline of an enclosure, a link in a chain, or prison cell. It is usually bad in situations and denotes delays, setbacks, or bindings. Astrologically it is associated with Capricorn and Saturn retrograde; Its

element is earth. It refers to immobility, and also thereby strength. Depending on the question it could indicate a restriction or a source of willpower. It is generally unfavorable, but can be favorable in questions involving stability or security. It is associated with the deities Saturn and Vesta, and the angels Cassiel and Hanael. It is associated with the knees and skeletal system of the body.

Conjunctio (Conjunction)

  Other names: association, bier.
  Meaning: combination of forces, for good or ill.

The figure resembles a crossroads or joining of two figures. The sign is neutral in meaning but good with joining or recovering things, especially marriage or relationships. Astrologically it is associated with Virgo and Mercury retrograde. It represents a combination of forces, for good or ill. By itself, it is neutral, only becoming favorable or not by other figures around it. Its element is air. It is associated with the deities Mercury and Ceres, and the angels Raphael and Hamaliel. It is associated with the intestines and digestive system.

Laetitia (Joy)

  Other names: bearded, laughing, singing, high tower, head lifted, candelabrum, high mountain, old man.

Meaning: happiness and health.

The figure resembles an arch, fountain, or rainbow. It is good in situations that concern potential, joy, or happiness. Astrologically it is associated with Pisces and Jupiter retrograde. Its element is fire. It is a positive figure for nearly all questions, representing fast situations and construction. It indicates upward motion, happiness, or joy. It is associated with the deities Jove and Neptune, and the angels Sachiel and Barchiel. It is associated with the feet.

Tristitia (Sorrow)
Other names: crosswise, diminished, head down, fallen tower.
Meaning: sorrow, suffering, illness and pain.

The figure resembles a broken arch or a stake being driven into the ground. It is bad in most cases and connotes sadness or mourning. Astrologically it is associated with Aquarius and Saturn. Tristitia is an unfavorable figure in almost all questions, usually representing pain and suffering. However, it is favorable in questions dealing with stability, building, or the Earth such as agriculture. Its element is earth. It is associated with the deities Saturn and Juno, and the angels Cassiel and Gabriel. It is associated with the ankles and lower legs.

Rubeus (Red)
Other names: burning.
Meaning: passion, vice, fierceness, a hot temper.
The figure is an overturned glass; an inversion. Like the Tail of the Dragon, the figure is considered so unfavorable that if it were the first in a reading, the reading would end. Astrologically it is associated with Scorpio and Mars retrograde; Its element is air. It represents passion, deception, violence, and vice. It is associated with the god Mars, and the angels Samael and Barbiel. It is associated with the reproductive and excretory systems along with the genitals.

Albus (White)
Meaning: peace, wisdom, purity; a favorable figure, but weak.

The figure resembles an upright glass or goblet. It is good in most situations, especially with good figures in company, but itself is a weak figure. Astrologically it is associated with Gemini and Mercury; Is inner element is water. It represents peace, wisdom and purity. It benefits beginnings and profit, or any situation where careful and deliberate planning is needed. It is associated with the deities Mercury and Apollo, and the angels Raphael and Ambriel. It is associated with the shoulders and lungs.

Fortuna Minor (Lesser Fortune)
Other names: outer help, protection going out, lesser omen, outer honor, apparent honor.
Meaning: good fortune, especially for endings; swiftness.

The figure is symbolic of success coming down like beams of light from the Sun. Astrologically it is associated with Leo and the Sun. Its elemental ruler is fire. It indicates a weakly positive outcome in nearly all questions, representing transient success that is dependent upon outside help. It favors situations that can be resolved quickly and do not need to be sustained. It is a figure of change and instability. It is associated with the deities Apollo and Jupiter, and the angels Michael and Verchiel. It is associated with the spine.

Fortuna Major (Greater Fortune)
Other names: inner help, protection going in, greater omen, inner honor.
Meaning: great good fortune, especially for

beginnings.

The figure resembles blessings growing from the earth and being fruitful in the air. It is good in all situations. A best case scenario. It represents great good fortune, especially in beginnings. Astrologically it is associated with Leo, and with the Sun in northern declinations. Its element is earth. It denotes power and success, and so is very favorable in conflicts and contests; being a figure of stability and long-term success, it also denotes hardship at the outset of an endeavor. It is associated with the deities Apollo and Jupiter, and the angels Michael and Verchiel. It is associated with the heart and chest.

Populus (People)
♦ ♦ Other names: congregation, multitude, double
♦ ♦ path.
♦ ♦
♦ ♦ Meaning: multitude; a neutral figure.

The figure resembles a bird's eye view of a group of people. The figure can mean that the outcome is based on the people of the situation, or represents a large number of people or peers. Astrologically it is associated with Cancer and the waxing Moon; Its element is water. It refers to a gathering or assembly of people and is very neutral, for though there may be a great deal of movement within the crowd, there is very little effect on the crowd as a whole. It is favorable with favorable figures, and unfavorable with unfavorable ones. It is associated with the deities Diana and Mercury, and the angels Gabriel and Muriel. It is associated with the breasts and torso.

Geomancy Methods

Generating the Geomantic Chart
Geomancy requires the geomancer to create sixteen lines of points or marks without counting, creating sixteen random numbers.

Quick Method
Traditionally, geomancy requires a surface of sand over which the point of a long stick is bounced to produce dots. dice or other objects are thrown; the eyes on potatoes are counted, or beans are drawn from a sack.

The number of dots or object are then counted; an odd number gave a single dot, an even result two dots, and this was taken as the head of the first figure. Another line was made to produce the neck, another for the body, and finally the feet

◆ head - fire
◆ neck - air
◆ ◆ body - water
◆ feet - earth

Each figure has four lines or rows, with each row representing one of the elements; each row can be either active or passive. Puer is here shown to have the Fire, Air, and Earth lines active, but the Water line remains passive.

Active, as the Yang in the I-Ching, is masculine and Passive, as with Yin, is considered feminine. This can also be referred to as *stable* or *mobile*. In simple "yes or no" style divinations, stable figures indicate a positive answer, while mobile figures indicate a negative one. The passive or active quality of a figure can also represent the duration of its effect. A stable quality will represent a long-term situation or that a certain object remains where it was left, while a mobile figure represents something that is transient or changing.

Quality	Figures
Stable	Acquisitio, Albus, Puella, Populus, Tristitia, Caput Draconis, Carcer, Fortuna Major
Mobile	Laetitia, Cauda Draconis, Amissio, Fortuna Minor, Rubeus, Puer, Conjunctio, Via

A quick geomantic divination is produced by generating one figure by any of the random methods mentioned at the start of this section and then interpreting just that one symbol. Each geomantic figure represents a certain state of the world or the mind, and can be interpreted in various ways based upon the query put forth and the method used to generate the figures.
- Basic meaning
- Gender
- Elemental attribution
- Astrological association

The 16 figures are split into 4 sets of 4 elemental symbols as seen below:-

Element	Figures Ruled
Fire	Laetitia, Cauda Draconis, Fortuna Minor, Amissio
Air	Puer, Rubeus, Acquisitio, Conjunctio
Water	Populus, Via, Albus, Puella
Earth	Fortuna Major, Tristitia, Caput Draconis, Carcer

The 16 figures are further co-related to the planets:-

Planet	Positive	Negative
Sun	Fortuna Major	Fortuna Minor
Moon	Populus	Via
Mercury	Albus	Conjunctio
Venus	Puella	Amissio
Mars	Puer	Rubeus
Jupiter	Acquisitio	Laetitia
Saturn	Tristitia	Carcer
Lunar nodes	Caput Draconis	Cauda Draconis

And co-related to their astrological attributions:-

Astrological Sign	Geomancy Symbol
Aries:	Puer
Taurus:	Amissio
Gemini:	Albus
Cancer:	Populus, Via
Leo:	Fortuna Major, Fortuna Minor
Virgo:	Coniunctio
Libra:	Puella
Scorpio:	Rubeus
Sagittarius:	Acquisitio
Capricorn:	Career
Aquarius:	Tristitia
Pisces:	Laetitia

The list of attributions is large and some of them obscure or culturally dependent - these lists represent just some of the more common allocations of meaning for simple geomancy divination.

The Shield
The shield chart is the most commonly used geomancy method and provides much more detail about the situation or question than the quick method. The geomantic figures generated are entered into a specialized table, shown here known as the shield chart.

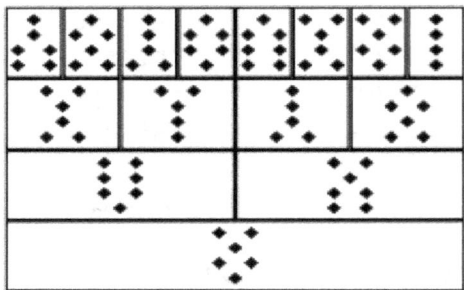

A total of sixteen such lines had to be drawn to produce the first four figures, the Four Mothers.
The first four figures, called the Mothers, form the basis for the rest of the figures in the chart; they occupy the first four houses in the upper right-hand corner The Daughters are placed in the next four houses in order on the same row as the Mothers.

The next four figures are the Daughters. The First Daughter is produced by taking formed by taking the first line or head of each of the Four Mothers in order:, thus the head of the First Mother becomes the First Daughter's head; the head of the Second Mother becomes the First Daughter's neck; the head of the Third Mother becomes the First Daughter's body, and the head of the Fourth Mother becomes the First Daughter's feet. In the same way, the necks of the Mothers produce the Second Daughter, their bodies the Third Daughter, and their feet the Fourth Daughter.

```
         Daughters                    Mothers
     X X   X X   X X   X  X      X  X X   X X   X
     X X   X     X     X  X X    X  X     X     X
     X     X     X  X  X X X X   X  X     X     X
     X X   X     X     X          X         X      X
      4     3     2     1          4     3     2     1
```

To produce the First Niece from the First and Second Mothers, the points in the heads, necks, bodies and feet of these two Mothers are added together. If the number of points in the heads of the Mothers comes to an even number, the head of the Niece is a double point; if it comes to an odd number, the Niece's head is a single point. The same process is done with the rest of the two Mothers, as shown below.

```
     X    X + X    even + even =  =    X  X
     X    X   X         even             X
     X    X   X    even + odd = odd      X
       X    X   X  odd + even = odd    X  X
       2      1    odd + odd = even   First Niece
```

In the same way, the Third and Fourth Mothers produce the Second Niece, the First and Second Daughters the Third Niece, and the Third and Fourth Daughters the Fourth Niece.

This additive process continues, giving rise to three more figures: the Witnesses and the Judge. The Right Witness is created in exactly the same way from the First and Second Nieces, and the Left Witness from the Third and Fourth Nieces. Finally, the Judge is created by adding together the Witnesses according to the same process. The result is shown below.

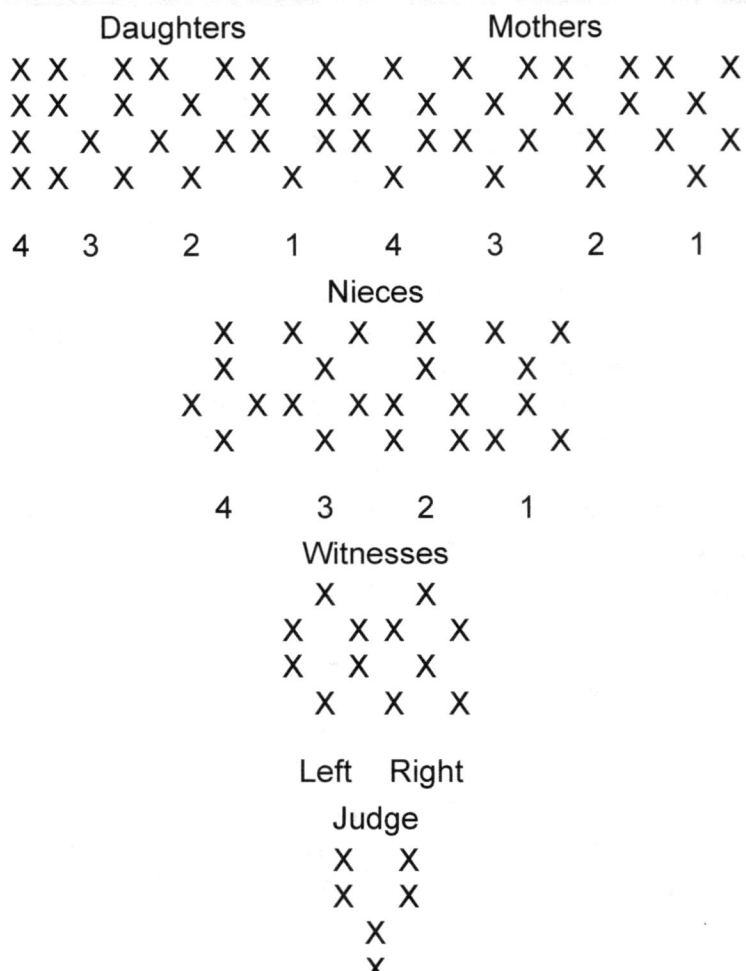

At the end of this process, the complete geomantic chart has been produced, and the mechanical part of geomantic divination is finished. What remains is the interpretation of the chart, where the patterns that have come out of this first phase become bearers of meaning.

The Judge the most significant, and it's possible to get a fairly clear idea of the basic outcome of the reading by taking the Judge alone as a guide.

The two Witnesses, the figures from which the Judge is produced, add an additional level of meaning. A favorable Judge derived from two favorable Witnesses is made more positive still, while an unfavorable Judge derived from two unfavorable Witnesses is the worst possible sign. A Judge, favorable or unfavorable, which is produced from one favorable and one unfavorable Witness takes on a middle significance, representing a situation in which good and ill are combined. A favorable Judge coming from this combination often means success, but with difficulty and delay; an unfavorable Judge from the same situation often means failure, but with some mitigating factors.

A favorable Judge which derives from two unfavorable Witnesses becomes unfavorable, although not extremely so; it often means a seemingly unfortunate turn of events which comes out for the best in the long run. An unfavorable Judge which derives from two favorable Witnesses becomes somewhat favorable, although it can often mean a success which has negative consequences in the end. In all cases, the meaning of the figures themselves should be carefully studied, as these provide the context in which these favorable or unfavorable indications take shape.

There is also an element of time in these relationships. The Right Witness is said to represent the past of the question, the Left Witness the future, while the Judge represents the situation in its broadest sense, including past, present and future. Thus, for example, a favorable Judge derived from an unfavorable First Witness and a favorable Left Witness represents a turn for the better, in which past difficulties are left behind; the same Judge derived from a favorable Right Witness and an unfavorable Left Witness stands for a situation in which past and present successes will be paid for with future trouble.

One division of the shield chart for interpretation involves triplets of the figures called triplicities. Each triplicity contains two of the Mothers or two of the Daughters and the Niece that results from them. They can be interpreted in a manner similar to the Witnesses and Judge, in that the right parent represents the past, the child the present, and the left parent the future; another way to interpret such a triplet views the right parent as the querent's side, allies, resources, and opinions, the left parent as the question's side, and the child as the interaction of the two sides.

"It was the hour when the diurnal heat no more can warm the coldness of the moon, vanquished by earth, or peradventure Saturn. When geomancers their Fortuna Major see in the orient before the dawn rise by a path that long remains not dim..." —Dante Aligheri, referencing the Greater Fortune (Fortuna Major) and the Way ("the path")

Geomancy diagram credits: Tascil, Wikimedia Commons. Public Domain.

Geomancy method explanation derived from John Michael Greer http://hermetic.com/caduceus/articles/2/2/medieval-methods-of-geomancy.html - a public domain website

Triplicity	Figures Involved	Interpretation
First Triplicity	First Mother, Second Mother, First Niece	The querent's health, disposition, outlooks, and habits. Current trends in the querent's life.
Second Triplicity	Third Mother, Fourth Mother, Second Niece	The influences in the querent's life at the time of the reading. Factors that shape the querent's life and the situation surrounding the query.
Third Triplicity	First Daughter, Second Daughter, Third Niece	The places most frequented by the querent, including the home and the workplace. People and objects found at those places. Family, partners, and housemates of the querent.
Fourth Triplicity	Third Daughter, Fourth Daughter, Fourth Niece	Friends, associates, coworkers, colleagues of the querent, as well as people in authority over the querent. Situations and factors caused by external sources.

Common Symbols
& Their Meanings

These are the most common subconscious archetype symbols. Their interpretations are meant as a starting point and will vary in their personal meaning, depending upon the individual's information filters and reality tunnel. These symbols can also be used to discover the meaning in dreams. Many people find that their dreams become more vivid and easier to remember as they begin scrying. The universe uses dreams to double confirm messages that you are trying to receive because you are now more open and receptive to listening to the message given.

I recommend keeping a personal journal of your dreams, divinations and scrying sessions for four reasons:-
1) So that you can more easily refer your entries to the lists in this book until you become familiar with the basic symbology.
2) You will see which methods work best for you.
3) When your insight and predictions come true you can refer to the entry, page and date. This will give you confidence in the methods that you are using successfully.
4) So that you can see how to fine tune your intuitive interpretations with the actual outcomes.

As you do this you will be learning the intimate details of the universal language. You will become a skilled translator of the universal language into your native tongue and deliver clearer messages that will benefit yourself and those that seek your help as a scryer.

Acorn - at the top means success and gain: at the bottom means good health.

Aircraft - journey; if broken means danger of accident; can also mean a rise in position

Anchor - at top rest, stability, constancy; at bottom means clouded, inconstancy

Animals - instinctive part of self attuned to nature and survival (survival in the social world). Animals sometimes represents one's parents, especially their relationship to a parent (love, hate, etc.). Being chased by an animal may represent some repressed emotion or aggression. Look at the particular animal to determine the symbol it may represent.

Apple - achievement

Axe - difficulties; if at top overcoming of difficulties

Baby - small worries - may symbolize vulnerability, or your need for love. Also your pure, innocent, true self (other than the ego). It may represent some new development in your life. A baby commonly appears in the dreams of pregnant women and may be a straightforward expression of pregnancy.

Bag - a trap; if open, escape

Ball - variable fortunes

Bats - good weather the next day - See section on the "Language of the Bat"

Bell - unexpected news; good if near top

Birds - good news - See the section on "Augury"

Boat - visit from a friend, protection

Book - if open it's good news; if closed you need to investigate something

Bush - new friend or opportunities

Butterfly - fickleness

Cabbage - jealousy; with dots means at work

Candle - help from others

Cap - trouble

Cat - Pleasure, deceit, a false friend -

Chain - engagement, a wedding

Chair - a guest

Changing your clothes - may indicate a change in your lifestyle (past, present or future)

Cigar - a new friend

Circle - success, completion; with dots means a baby

Clock - better health

Clothes - clothes may represent your persona, how you look at yourself and how you feel others may see you. Old and worn out clothes mat symbolize anxiety about your attractiveness or you need to discard some habitual way of thinking. Clothes in a dream being worn by someone else may suggests that there is some part of you that you relate to in that particular person. See naked listed below.

Clouds - trouble; with dots means many problems

Coin - money coming

Comb - an enemy

Cross - represents perfect balance (as in the christ within or buddha consciousness). It may be a symbol for a crossroads in your life or a burden to heavy to carry. It also may be a symbol of death, something coming to an end in your life (relationships, job, change of lifestyle, etc).
Cross - suffering, sacrifice

Cup - reward

Dagger - danger from self or others; beware

Dead person - in a dream may relate to past relationships with that particular person. If the dead person is you then consider your true condition as you see it, i feel dead because of my job, life, relationships, etc. Or death may simply represent your anxiety about dying

Death - death or dying in a death most often represents changes in one's life, something is coming to an end. Very seldom does death symbolize true dying of a person. The old is dying and with the death of the old comes new beginnings. The death and resurrection of christ is a good example in mythology of the death motif. What it represents is the death of the ego-self and its resurrection to a spiritual realization.

Devil - evil spirits, not necessarily religious. It may represent some repressed emotions that need to be expressed. It may symbolize a need to change one's behavior (devilish) and find a spiritual center.

Dish - trouble at home

Dog - good friend; if at bottom friend needs help

Door - odd event

Duck - money coming

Egg - good omen

Elephant - wisdom and strength

Envelope - good news

Eye - caution

Face a change, may be a setback

Falling - may represent your real life fear of letting go of something or someone. It also may suggest a loss of control in a situation. Self-inflation is another possibility. Are you above yourself and due a fall?

Fan - flirtation

Feather - lack of concentration

Fence - limitations, minor setbacks, not permanent

Finger - emphasizes whatever sigh it points at

Fire - at top achievement; at bottom danger of haste

Fish - good fortune

Flag - danger

Fly - domestic annoyance

Food - represents knowledge. Physically food nourishes the body. Mentally knowledge nourishes the mind, thus the old adage of "food for thought".

Fork - false flattery

Forked line - decision

Fruit - prosperity

Gate - opportunity, future success

Glass - integrity

Glow - a challenge

Goat - be careful of enemies

Grapes - happiness

Gun - anger

Hair - represents knowledge, most often conscious knowledge (or the lack of). Abundant hair may signify virility or male sexuality (freud). Cutting hair may symbolize loss of virility, or castration. Loss of hair may express a fear of getting old or being unwanted.

Hammer - hard work needed

Hand - if open means friendship; if closed means an argument

Hands - symbolize ability, particularly practical and social abilities. Tied hands represent a feeling of an inability to succeed in a particular endeavor. Washing your hands often symbolizes guilt- what are you trying to get rid of?

Harp - love, harmony
Hat - improvement, especially in a new job

Hawk - jealousy

Heart - pleasure, love, trust
Horse - if galloping means good news; if just the head means a lover

Horseshoe - good luck

Hourglass - need to decide something

House - a symbol representing yourself. The rooms or different floors may represent emotions, attitudes, complexes, ideas. Going upstairs symbolizes conscious thinking. The basement represents the deep unconscious.

House - security

Iceberg - danger

Insect - problems are minor and you will easily overcome

Jewels - gifts

Kangaroo - harmony at home

Kettle - any illness is minor

Killing - may represent repression/suppression of some aspect of yourself - you want or need to kill that part of your personality. May indicate hatred or envy between siblings or hostility towards some person. Also putting an end to negative feelings or unwanted situations in one's life.

Kite - wishes coming true

Knife - broken friendship

Ladder - promotion, a rise in life

Lamp - at the top means a feast; at the side means secrets revealed; at the bottom means postponement

Leaf - new life

Letter - news

Lines - if straight means progress; if wavy means uncertain path

Lion - influential friends

Lock - obstacles

Loop - avoid impulsive actions

Man - near handle means a visitor

Marriage - a blending of intellectual and intuitive parts or masculine and feminine aspects of oneself. A bridge between the conscious mind and the unconscious self (as in dreams).

Mask - excitement; insecurity

Money - represents one's values in life. May symbolize self worth. In exchanging money, it may represent changes about to happen in your life. Take note of any numbers and find their meaning(s). For instance, five often symbolizes changes in life.

Mountain - great goals but with many difficulties. Climbing a mountain may symbolize achievements or tasks to be performed. Looking from a mountain may symbolize your life under review, without the conscious emotional involvement (dreams looks at your life without prejudices). A mountain may represent obstacles in your life.

Mouse - theft - See Section on "Myomancy"

Mushroom - at top means journey or moving to the country; near bottom means rapid growth; if reversed means frustration

Nail - injustice, unfairness

Naked - being nude may symbolize the 'naked truth' about oneself. Totally open and exposed. It may be an expression for childhood innocence and freedom from artificial inhibitions. Showing off your nudity may be a desire for sex, or a desire for recognition.

Necklace - complete, admirers; if broken means danger of losing a lover

Needle - recognition, admiration

Oak - health, long life

Octopus - danger

Ostrich - travel

Owl - not keeping secrets, gossip, scandal

Palm tree - success, honor

Parasol - new lover

Parrot - a journey, but also can mean people talking

People - most often represents the different aspects of oneself; emotions, attitudes, desires, fears, etc. Look to the particular characteristics of a person or persons in the dream.

Pig - greed

Pistol - danger

Purse - at top means profit; at bottom means loss

Question mark - need for caution

Rabbit - need for bravery

Radio - communication between conscious and unconscious self (as in dream). Communications (or lack of) between aspects of self or between persons in your life.

Rake - watch details

Raven - bad news

Ring - at top means marriage or the offer of marriage; at bottom means long engagement; if broken means engagement broken off

Roads - your direction in life, the road you are following (may need changing or modifications). Patterns in your life, something that you continually do that may be harmful or unnecessary. Goals in life. What is your path in life?

Rose - popularity

Saw - interference

Scale - legal issues; if balanced means just result; if unbalanced means unjust result

School - lessons in life. Self understanding is learning to know yourself (psychological). Life's experiences. Have you learned from them or do you ignore what is evident for what is convenient?

Scissors - quarrels, possibly separation

Sex - may symbolize a unification of unconscious aspects in your life to a conscious realization. Uniting parts of oneself that was previously separated due to repression/suppression. May be a straight forward desire for sex. Uninhibited sex may suggest one's actual persona is uninhibited.

Sheep - good fortune

Shell - good news

Shelter - danger of loss or ill health

Ship - worthwhile journey

Shoe, new - change for the better

Shoe, old - stability and comfort

Snake - an enemy, but also wisdom

Spider - reward for work

Spoon - generosity

Star - health and happiness, hope

Sun - happiness, success, power

Sword - arguments

Table - social gatherings

Teacher - a symbol for your higher self (spiritual or creative). Insights that show you the way on your path.

Teeth - assimilating of knowledge (unconscious) so to understand and make use of it.losing teeth symbolizes change in one's way of thinking. Also symbolizes a fear of getting old. May symbolize aggression.

Tent - travel

Thimble - changes at home

Tortoise - criticism, usually beneficial

Tower - disappointment

Tree - improvements

Triangle - something unexpected

Umbrella - annoyances

Urn - wealth and happiness

Vase - a friend needs help

Vehicles - a symbol representing yourself. Are you driving (in control), in the back or passenger seat (not in control). Is your mother driving? Perhaps she has too much control of your life. A bus may symbolize yourself and the passengers aspects of your personality.

Violin - egotism

Volcano - harmful emotions

Wagon - a wedding

Wasp - romantic problems

Water - water represents the unconscious self (mind). Pools of water, lakes, rivers, symbolize the personal unconscious, whereas oceans and seas represent the deeper collective (universal) unconscious.

Waterfall - prosperity

Wheel - if complete means good fortune; if broken means disappointment

Wings - messages

Wolf - jealousy

Yoke - domination

Zebra - adventure, especially overseas

It wont be long before your craving an understanding of the more complex universal symbology.

A study of tarot symbolism will open a deeper understanding of the more complex metaphorical language of the universe to the serious student.

When the student is ready the teacher is here.

Contact the author above at the website below if you wish to enroll for her courses or would like a catalog of her other books

http://www.happymediumpublishing.org
http://www.shambhallah.org
http://www.magick.org.au

www.ingramcontent.com/pod-product-compliance
Lightning Source LLC
Chambersburg PA
CBHW070626300426
44113CB00010B/1677